Other Books by Robin Rask

Robin's Simple Recipe for Finding a Job!

Self-Management to Time Management

Work Ethics and the Generation Gap!

Maybe more to come …

STEPS TO EMPLOYMENT AND SUCCESS

ROBIN RASK

authorHOUSE®

AuthorHouse™
1663 Liberty Drive
Bloomington, IN 47403
www.authorhouse.com
Phone: 1 (800) 839-8640

Published by AuthorHouse   12/30/2016

ISBN: 978-1-5246-5001-8 (sc)
ISBN: 978-1-5246-5000-1 (e)

Library of Congress Control Number: 2016919017

Print information available on the last page.

Any people depicted in stock imagery provided by Thinkstock are models,
and such images are being used for illustrative purposes only.
Certain stock imagery © Thinkstock.

This book is printed on acid-free paper.

Because of the dynamic nature of the Internet, any web addresses or links contained in this book may have changed
since publication and may no longer be valid. The views expressed in this work are solely those of the author and do
not necessarily reflect the views of the publisher, and the publisher hereby disclaims any responsibility for them.

To all those who may be seeking

employment, success, time-management skills, and

enhancing their customer service skills.

Contents

Preface xi

Acknowledgments xiii

Introduction xv

Chapter 1: How to Find a Job 1

- Three Simple Steps to Persuade Someone to Hire You 2
- Assessments 3
- How to Dress for Your Job Search 9
- Sources of Employment 11
- Master Application 12
- How to Find a Job 14
- Robin's Simple Recipe 17
- Robin's One-Page Recipe for Finding a Job 18
- Job Leads Log Sheet 20
- Employer Online Testing 24
- Informational Interviews 27
- Informational Interview Worksheets 32
- Job Shadowing 35
- Employer Phone Interview 36
- Networking 38
- 100 Ways to Motivate Yourself 40
- Success Is … 43

Chapter 2: Interviews 44

- Three Things That Make a Good Impression during an Interview 45
- The Job Interview and First Impressions 46
- Preparing for the Interview 48
- Personal Strengths 50
- Some Common Interview Questions 52
- Questions You May Want to Ask 54

- Practice Interview Questions 55
- Mock Interview Rating Questions 58
- Preparing for the Actual Interview 60
- Why People May Not Get Hired 66
- If You're Offered the Job 68
- Sample Thank-You Letter 70
- Sample Letter of Resignation 71
- Follow-Ups after the Application, Résumé, and Interview 72
- Smiling Facts 75

Chapter 3:   Résumé 76

- How to Compose Your Résumé 77
- Preparing Your Résumé 78
- Résumé Sample: Completed Outline / Functional Format 82
- Résumé Chronological Format 85
- Résumé Key Phrases 88
- Action Words 89
- Résumé Writing Skills 91
- Scannable Résumé 93
- Résumé Sample: Scannable Format 94
- Work Portfolio 95
- Personal References 96
- Letters of Recommendation 98
- Sample Letter of Recommendation 98
- Sample Cover Letter 99
- A Poem for Computer Users over Forty 100

Chapter 4:   Work Ethics 102

- What Is or Are Work Ethics? 103
- Ten+ Most Wanted List 107
- More Employer Expectations 109
- Employer Feedback 112
- An Employer's Perspective 114
- The Three D's To Motivation 116
- TEAM and Team Building 117

- Time Management 119
- Instructions for Time-Management Chart 125
- Time-Management Chart 126
- Stress and Burnout 128
- Holiday Stress Busters 132
- How to Make New Year's Resolutions Stick 133
- Coping with Anxiety and Stress 134
- Example Letter of Resignation 135
- Leaving Your Job? 136
- The ABCs of Loving Your Job 137
- Love what you do, or do something else. 138
- Ten Simple Ways to Lose Your Job 139
- Getting to Know the Job 140
- Getting Along on the Job 142
- Qualities of a Leader 144
- America's Drug Problem 146

Chapter 5: Customer Service 148

- Providing Excellent Customer Service 150
- Customer Complaints 151
- What Is Customer Service and How Important Is It? by Michael Stevens 152
- Ten Things to Remember about Customers, ... 159
- "I Am Your Customer" 160
- Treating Customers Well 161
- 14 Steps to Success 164
- Pencils 166

Chapter 6: Goal Setting and Affirmations 167

- Goals 168
- You Are So Blessed 169
- Famous People with Learning Disorders and Other Disabilities 170
- Five Steps to Build Self-Esteem 172
- Affirmations 173
- Goals 174
- Former Presidents 178

- The Farmer and His Donkey 179
- Positive Affirmations 180
- Some Keys to Success..183
- Important Goals by Category..186
- Vision Board or Book 188
- Bill Bartmann's Nine Steps to Achieve Any Goal 189
- Guiding Questions in Assisting Someone to Pursue Their Dreams by Denise Bissonette 190
- Three Ways to Change Your Life..192

Chapter 7: Employment and Educational Resources 193

- Tips for Participating in Job Fairs..194
- Apprenticeship Information 196
- Hospital-Based Health Care Careers to Consider 199
- Menu of Jobs Available in the Restaurant Industry 204
- Farmers Insurance..206
- Guard Cards 208
- Questions and Answers about ROP 209
- California Picture ID Cards 210
- CAL Grants: Money for College 212
- Employment City 214
- Employment Websites: Local and Inland Area and More 217
- California Jobs, Websites, and Resources..230
- Military and California Conservation Corps Information....................240

Preface

I have been assisting students and adults as a job developer / employment specialist and ROP instructor with jobs and employment skills for more than twenty-six years. Many things I have learned by trial and error and then made a career out of it. This allows me to share my experience and resources with everyone who may benefit from them. I have assembled similar curriculum guide workbooks for students and adults. In addition, I have taught all these skills in the classroom. Therefore, I want to share this with all who may be seeking employment in order to help them become more successful.

I have a personnel administrative credential along with lifelong experience. In the past fifteen years, I have seen a significant difference in our youth, graduates, and adult generation, and it is not for the better. Therefore, I wrote the book *Work Ethics and the Generation Gap* in 2008. What the community has to say is in chapter 7; it is a must-read. The book also includes a section on the German school system. In Germany, students come out of school ready to go to work or into a trade. There is no welfare.

Many people are going with the flow while trying to keep up with all the latest and not-always-all-the-greatest technology and other stuff, not realizing the negative influence we are modeling for our children. When we spoil our children too much and neglect to teach them responsibilities, they become what we taught them. Some graduates don't want to work or go to school and stay home as long as they can. Technically, once a child turns eighteen, parents are no longer responsible for him or her. These teens are adults and should be preparing for their adult lives, as we all had to. However, if some graduates want to go to college and their parents allow them to live at home, the parents can claim them on their taxes till the day before they turn twenty-six years old.

When I grew up, we could not wait to turn sixteen to get our driver's licenses and made plans to move out. I, along with many, grew up in a time where there were no computers or cell phones. That may be why our generation is more responsible and productive. Of course, we then passed those work ethics on to our kids, and they will do the same with their children. It all begins with good parenting, and it is never too late for that. We all need to be positive, productive role models for our children, students, and others.

> Train a child in the way he should go, and when he is old he will not turn from it (Proverbs 22:6 NIV)

When it comes to teaching students and adults how to find a job, I am blunt and to the point because I am very passionate and want them to obtain employment and become successful. Some students have said that I scare them. But I give them the facts and what employers expect. I tell my applicants, "If you are not going to include all the steps and do it all the way, then do not look for a job at all." Otherwise it ends up being a waste of time. It is similar to going on a diet. You will either follow the plan to lose the weight or you will not.

When it comes to success, it is not always about money and having large homes and all the toys. It is more about motivation, dedication, discipline, overcoming obstacles, and learning to say no to things that do not produce good fruit in our lives. Because that is what will get us closer to the things we want and need.

Having a job and your needs met and the ability to pay your bills and being happy is considered success, along with having someone special to share it with. It is also important to enjoy what you do and are good at it. God gave us all gifts and talents and ordained us to work.

I am still an author in progress. Like everything else in life, the more time we devote to our talents and passion, the better we become. We need to pray and listen to God for our purpose in life. Then things eventually fall into place.

I wanted to have this resource available *to all* who may benefit from the information.

I strongly believe in sharing information that can benefit others. Whenever I hear people talking about needing a job, I try to give them information to assist them. I also belong to a job-developer network group, and we have quarterly meetings and e-mail jobs to one another almost daily. We then send those job leads out to others. Many of those people then forward those job leads to the people they know who need a job. Most of us know someone who needs a job.

I would be honored to see this resource guide utilized by as many people and schools as possible because I believe it will give them a step up toward their future and success. Part of life is paying it forward; writing these books is my way. In addition, they make great gifts!

Thank you, good luck, and Godspeed!

Acknowledgments

I want to thank all the student workers in my office who have assisted with some of the flyers and retyping of some of the documents throughout the years. I greatly appreciate it! I also want to thank SBCSS for giving me the opportunity to work with all the different programs to assist students in becoming employed and more successful.

Also want to give a big thank-you to all those who shared their information for this guide. It is greatly appreciated.

I may not be a famous author, but I strongly believe that God has inspired and directed me to write the books I have written and continue to write to help make a difference in others' lives. And I pray that it does.

I continue to thank and praise God for all he has done and continues to do in my life despite my challenges. Good things are on the way because with God all things are possible.

Mathew 19:26

Introduction

This book is written and designed to help anyone who needs a job. In addition, I suggest using it in classrooms to assist students with transitioning from school to work. This guide provides examples of how to find a job, fill out applications, go through interviews, write résumés, set goals, and use affirmations to become more successful. It may also help businesses and young workers to provide better customer service.

Steps to Employment and Success will also assist with work ethics, networking, time management, and self-esteem. It also includes an array of resources and where to find jobs.

Tools needed for obtaining employment are

- researching a company you might want to work for;
- persistence and professionalism;
- networking;
- a pen with an eraser;
- an updated résumé;
- a portfolio of your accomplishments;
- a completed sample application;
- preparation to complete and pass online assessments;
- appropriate interview clothing;
- ability to communicate your strengths and skills;
- confidence and good manners;
- actually going to the business and introducing yourself;
- transportation;
- a social security card and ID;
- keeping a log of where you go, who you saw, and what was said;
- sending thank-you notes or letters after the interview; and
- following up.

This is all covered in this guide—and more!

There is no reason for anyone who wants to work and is capable of working to not have a job. If there is a need, there is a job!

My *Work Ethics* book should be flying off the shelves, but not everyone wants to work. That may be why there are so many homeless people standing on street corners holding cardboard signs begging for food. Then again, for some that is their job and their choice. It is difficult to know who is sincere and who is scamming us. I usually keep job information and treats in my car, and when the impulse strikes me, I throw them out the window to bless them.

Robin's Simple Recipe for Finding a Job is just that. If people truly want to work, it could be the ticket for obtaining employment. It has all the tools needed and is only ninety-seven pages, with a one-page recipe to obtaining a job that is also included in this book. It is a much shorter version of this guide and is endorsed by author and speaker Hanoch McCarty.

I have read some similar books to those I have written. Though the information is great, some are just too long and hard to follow. I don't want to read a time-management book that is three hundred pages. I want the nuts and bolts. My time-management book is only sixty pages. Denise Bissonnette, author, job developer, poet, curriculum developer, and speaker, also endorsed the book.

The chapters of this guide are arranged in sections to assist with your job search and success. You may notice that some things are repeated, but they apply to those chapters. Feel free to copy any of the worksheets in this book.

When looking for a job you need the right tools, just like a mechanic needs to work on cars.

Chapter 1

How to Find a Job

Three Simple Steps

to Persuade Someone

to Hire You:

1) Look your best.

2) Be prepared and confident.

3) Show interest.

ASSESSMENTS

Many classrooms are using varies types of assessments and or career interest based surveys to determine what types of jobs and careers students may be interested in. Many of them are available through JIST.

Taking the assessments allows students to begin planning their classes for their future career goals. Once they know what type of job or career they want to pursue they can look them up in the Occupational Outlook Handbook and online. It is developed by the U.S. Department of Labor and usually updated every two years.

Information includes, Earnings, training, education, skills required, related jobs, work environment and job outlook.

I have been given permission to include an example of the Career Guide created by ROP. It is an oldie but a goodie. Just follow the instructions, then you can use the enclosed Research and Occupation form to look up the job in the Occupational Outlook Handbook. This is also a great classroom activity and the students can take turns reading their job / career out loud. The career they selected may spark another students interest.

JIST.com

(800) 328-1452

Name _____   Grade _____

San Bernardino County Superintendent of Schools
REGIONAL OCCUPATIONAL PROGRAM

CAREER GUIDE

Have you ever asked yourself what kind of jobs are available which match your interests and abilities? That can be a difficult task considering there are over forty thousand different jobs from which to choose – and the job scene is changing all the time.

This Career Guide was designed to help you begin to examine what career fields are best suited for you, and how you can take advantage of opportunities to explore a variety of jobs within these career fields.

Please read each statement below and check those that reflect how you feel.

CLUSTER A

Is it important for you to:
____ Influence the opinion of people through writing
____ Express ideas through drawing, painting, photography, etc.
____ Entertain others through dance, music or acting
____ Use your talent to decorate or create art objects

Have you enjoyed (or think you would enjoy) any of the following?
____ Writing original poems or stories
____ Taking photographs of family, friends, or activities
____ Drawing or painting
____ Acting in a play
____ Singing in a choir
____ Creating dance routines
____ Making your own jewelry

Have you liked and done well in any of the following school subjects?
____ English   ____ Art
____ Drama   ____ Speech
____ Journalism   ____ Music

Would you like to work in places such as:
____ Radio and television studios
____ Newspaper/magazine publishers
____ Theater and motion picture studios
____ Advertising agencies
____ Museums
____ Recording studios
____ Schools and colleges

[ ] Total checked

CLUSTER B

Is it important for you to:
____ Deal with people
____ Make decisions based on your own judgment
____ Speak and write concisely and clearly
____ Work in detail, computing and/or recording data accurately
____ Perform work that is routine and organized

Have you enjoyed (or think you would enjoy) any of the following?
____ Being a treasurer for a club or organization
____ Taking minutes at meetings or handling correspondence for an organization
____ Maintaining your families checking account
____ Helping conduct a school or community survey
____ Having a collection such as stamps or coins
____ Using a computer to organize and store data and write letters

Have you liked and done well in any of the following school subjects?
____ Typing   ____ Business Math
____ Shorthand   ____ Bookkeeping or Accounting
____ English   ____ Speech

Would you like to work in places such as:
____ Law offices   ____ Government agencies
____ Banks   ____ Small businesses
____ Accounting firms ____ Department Stores
____ Grocery stores

[ ] Total checked

CLUSTER C

Is it important for you to:
____ Help people who are sick or injured
____ Help people have a better life
____ Care for, and entertain children
____ Teach people to learn new skills or information

Have you enjoyed (or think you would enjoy) any of the following?
____ Applying first aid in emergencies
____ Coaching children or youth in sports or recreation activities
____ Helping conduct physical exercises for disabled persons
____ Nursing sick relatives and friends
____ Teaching games to children as a volunteer aide in a nursery school
____ Tutoring students in school subjects
____ Helping your friends or others solve personal problems

Have you liked and done well in any of the following school subjects?
____ Biology   ____ Physiology
____ Drama   ____ Psychology
____ Health Education ____ Speech

Would you like to work in places such as:
____ Doctor or dentist office
____ Sports facilities or health clubs
____ Hospitals
____ Day care centers
____ Mental health clinics
____ Social service agencies
____ Schools for special populations

[ ] Total checked

CLUSTER D

Is it important for you to:
____ Use your hands to do precision work
____ Direct and organize the work of others
____ Inspect things completely and accurately
____ Make or repair things using tools and machines
____ Check your work for accuracy and quality
____ Follow instructions carefully
____ See the results of your work

Have you enjoyed (or think you would enjoy) any of the following?
____ Assembling objects (i.e., bicycles, etc.) following drawings or written instructions
____ Being in charge of a group project
____ Operating machines or tools to complete tasks
____ Taking things apart to see how they work
____ Cleaning and maintaining tools and machines around your house

Have you liked and done well in any of the following school subjects?
____ General or   ____ Drafting
     Applied Math   ____ Geometry
____ Shop Classes   ____ Computers

Would you like to work in places such as:
____ Automobile production factories
____ Textile plants
____ Aircraft production factories
____ Warehouses
____ Welding shops
____ Printing shops
____ Furniture manufacturer

[ ] Total checked

CLUSTER E

Is it important for you to:

____ Use logic and scientific thinking to solve complex problems
____ Use computer technology
____ Teach others new skills
____ Gather, study, and analyze information
____ Defend the rights of people
____ Plan and direct the activities of others
____ Help others plan and manage their financial future
____ Promote ideas, people or products

Have you enjoyed (or think you would enjoy) any of the following?

____ Being a tutor
____ Visiting museums or historical sites
____ Being a president or treasurer of a club
____ Working on your school newspaper

Have you liked and done well in any of the following school subjects?

____ Mathematics   ____ Sociology/Psychology
____ English   ____ Accounting
____ Journalism

Would you like to work in places such as:

____ Banks/financial institutions   ____ Large businesses
____ Colleges   ____ Newspapers
____ Libraries/museums   ____ Schools and colleges
____ Law firms

[ ]   Total checked

CLUSTER F

Is it important for you to:

____ Use computers to store and organize information
____ Develop new and better ways of doing things
____ Design and build objects or structures
____ Make sure materials and products meet certain standards
____ Use hand tools and precision measuring instruments to make or repair things

Have you enjoyed (or think you would enjoy) any of the following?

____ Reading mechanical, automotive or computer magazines
____ Collecting and identifying rocks and minerals
____ Drawing detailed pictures of objects
____ Operating vehicles such as cars, trucks, boats, and airplanes
____ Working with your hands to repair things

Have you liked and done well in any of the following school subjects?

____ Metal/Wood Shop   ____ Mechanical Drawing/
____ Algebra   Drafting
____ Chemistry   ____ Electronics
____ Auto Mechanics   ____ Physics

Would you like to work in places such as:

____ Construction sites   ____ Trucking firms
____ Outdoors   ____ Factories
____ Airports   ____ Machine shops
____ Research laboratories

[ ]   Total checked

CLUSTER G

Is it important for you to:

____ Greet and get acquainted with people
____ Help people feel at ease in unfamiliar settings
____ Plan and direct social activities
____ Enhance the appearance of others

Have you enjoyed (or think you would enjoy) any of the following?

____ Planning and organizing a party
____ Teaching friends to dance
____ Being a treasurer or secretary for an organization
____ Cutting or styling your friends hair
____ Reading health and beauty magazines
____ Taking people on a trip
____ Being in charge of sports equipment for a team
____ Serving food to large groups of people

Have you liked and done well in any of the following school subjects?

____ Speech   ____ English
____ Drivers Education   ____ Mathematics

Would you like to work in places such as:

____ Airports   ____ Passenger ships
____ Restaurants   ____ Tour companies
____ Hotels   ____ Amusement parks
____ Barber or beauty shops   ____ Golf courses

[ ]   Total checked

CLUSTER H

Is it important for you to:

____ Compete with others in athletic or sporting events
____ Design a training program to prepare for a certain sport
____ Demonstrate athletic ability to entertain audiences
____ Make sure sporting event rules are being followed
____ Share your knowledge and abilities with others

Have you enjoyed (or think you would enjoy) any of the following?

____ Giving lessons to a group or individual
____ Coaching a sports team
____ Officiating at a sporting event
____ Competing in sports
____ Performing specialty acts such as juggling or acrobatics
____ Reading about sporting events or people

Have you liked and done well in any of the following school subjects?

____ Physical Education   ____ Health Science
____ Varsity Sports   ____ Physiology
____ English

Would you like to work in places such as:

____ Ski resorts
____ Sports arenas and stadiums
____ Athletic clubs
____ Circuses or carnivals
____ Rodeos
____ Schools or colleges
____ City recreation departments

[ ]   Total checked

CLUSTER I

Is it important for you to:

____ Plan and oversee the sales and shipment of farm crops or animals
____ Plant, cultivate, and harvest farm crops
____ Inspect plants for presence of insects or disease
____ Care for and/or train animals

Have you enjoyed (or think you would enjoy) any of the following?

____ Taking care of a sick or injured animal
____ Being a leader in scouting or other outdoor groups
____ Caring for your yard or garden
____ Raising small animals or fish
____ Training a pet such as a horse, bird or dog
____ Camping, hiking or hunting
____ Being a member of the Future Farmers of America (FFA)

Have you liked and done well in any of the following school subjects?

____ Plant Science   ____ Wood/Metal Shop
____ Biology   ____ Welding
____ Animal Science

Would you like to work in places such as:

____ Farm/ranch   ____ Fish hatchery
____ Park/forest preserve ____ Kennel
____ Zoo/aquarium   ____ Floral shop
____ Nursery (plants)   ____ Veterinary hospital

[ ] Total checked

CLUSTER J

Is it important for you to:

____ Help others facing emergencies
____ Protect the rights and property of others
____ Work under pressure or in the face of danger
____ Learn and enforce rules and procedures
____ Make conclusions based on facts and personal judgment
____ Pay attention to detail

Have you enjoyed (or think you would enjoy) any of the following?

____ Being a member of a volunteer fire department or emergency rescue squad
____ Hunting or target shooting
____ Reading detective stories or watching law or emergency type television shows
____ Taking first aid training

Have you liked and done well in any of the following school subjects?

____ Government/Civics   ____ Speech
____ Social Studies   ____ English
____ Health   ____ Science
____ Physical Education

Would you like to work in places such as:

____ Fire department   ____ National forest
____ Police department   ____ Jails or prisons
____ Factories or large retail stores (Security Guard)
____ FBI
____ Amusement establishments

[ ] Total checked

CLUSTER K

Is it important for you to:

____ Be able to organize your own activities
____ Express yourself clearly when talking with others
____ Help others make up their minds
____ Persuade or influence others

Have you enjoyed (or think you would enjoy) any of the following?

____ Selling items door to door to raise money for an organization
____ Making speeches or being on a debate team
____ Comparison shopping
____ Keeping accurate records as a treasurer for a club or organization
____ Designing ways to advertise an activity your organization is sponsoring
____ Organizing yard sales
____ Collecting money for charity

Have you liked and done well in any of the following school subjects?

____ English   ____ Business
____ Mathematics   ____ Accounting/Bookkeeping
____ Speech   ____ Psychology

Would you like to work in places such as:

____ Manufacturers   ____ Automobile agencies
____ Insurance companies ____ Door to door sales
____ Radio or television stations ____ Health industry
____ Department stores

[ ] Total checked

CLUSTER L

Is it important for you to:

____ Help solve environmental problems
____ Use advanced math to solve complex problems
____ Examine rock formations to develop theories about the earth and its history
____ Use microscopes to study cells
____ Heal sick or injured people
____ Develop ways to improve products

Have you enjoyed (or think you would enjoy) any of the following?

____ Reading magazines or books about scientific discoveries
____ Collecting rocks or minerals
____ Using a microscope to examine cells
____ Being a member of a scout or environmental group
____ Cultivating and caring for plants
____ Taking first aid training
____ Learning to recognize and identify different plants and animals
____ Amateur astronomy

Have you liked and done well in any of the following school subjects?

____ Advanced Mathematics ____ Biology
____ Physics   ____ Physiology/anatomy
____ Chemistry

Would you like to work in places such as:

____ Research laboratories ____ Observatories
____ Hospitals/Clinics   ____ Outdoors (mines, oil
____ Plant Nurseries   fields, lakes or oceans)

[ ] Total checked

• Write the total number of checked responses from each cluster in the corresponding boxes below.

A	B	C	D	E	F	G	H	I	J	K	L
[ ]	[ ]	[ ]	[ ]	[ ]	[ ]	[ ]	[ ]	[ ]	[ ]	[ ]	[ ]

• In which boxes (representing occupational clusters) do you have the highest numbers?
• Circle the boxes with the three highest numbers.
• On the next page you will find examples of occupations found in each cluster. Look at the clusters you circled to see what related occupations you have a preference for. You will be able to find more information on each occupation in your career center or library. Information can be found by occupational title or DOT number (9 digit number).

CAREER GUIDE CLUSTERS

Although there are many things to consider as you select a career, this guide will provide you with a start. We suggest that you visit your career center or see your ROP Recruitment Placement Specialist to find out more about the jobs listed in your preferred cluster.

Below are examples of related occupations and ROP classes by cluster. Taking an ROP class may be an excellent way to explore your career interests.

CLUSTER A - ARTISTIC - Related Occupations

- Actor/Actress
- Art Appraiser
- Audio/Visual Productions
- Cartoonist
- Casting Director
- Choral Director
- Choreographer
- Composer
- Critic
- Dancer
- Dance Studio Manager
- Disc Jockey/Broadcasting
- Engraver
- Fashion Artist
- Film Editor
- Floral Designer
- Furniture Designer
- Game Design
- Graphic Arts/Computer Tech.
- Illustrator
- Interior Designer
- Lyricist
- Merchandise Displayer
- Museum Tech.
- Musician
- Photographer
- Photojournalist
- Producer
- Prop Maker
- Quick Sketch Artist
- Screen Writer
- Set Illustrator
- Sound Technician
- Writer

Related ROP Courses

- Cosmetology
- Desktop Publishing
- Digital/Website Design, 3-D Anim.
- Floral Design & Sales
- Furniture/Cabinet Mfg./Finishing
- Graphic Communications
- Interior Design
- Machine Embroidery
- Manicuring - Nail Care
- Radio Broadcasting Occup.
- Recreation Occupations
- Silk Screening
- Stagecraft Construction /Design
- TV-Video Production

CLUSTER B - BUSINESS - Related Occupations

- Administrative Secretary
- Bookkeeper
- Cashier
- Claim Examiner
- Computer Occupations
- Dispatcher
- Eligibility Worker
- Financial Aid Counselor
- Fingerprint Clerk
- Hospitality Occupations
- Legal Secretary/Office Asst.
- Loan Counselor/Escrow
- Mailroom Supervisor
- Medical Records Tech.
- Medical Transcription
- Office Manager
- Payroll/Personnel Clerk
- Probation Officer
- Receptionist
- Registrar
- Reservation Agent
- Stenographer
- Teacher Aide
- Ticketing Clerk
- Traffic Manager
- Travel Agent
- Typist

Related ROP Courses

- Business Technology Lab
- Computer Business Applications
- Computer Game Design
- Computer Maintenance & Repair
- Computer Network Mgmt.
- Computer Sys. Protection/Security
- Computers - Intro. & Programming
- Desktop Publishing
- Entrepreneurship
- Financial Services Occupations
- Foundations of Info. Tech.
- Introduction to Computers
- Legal Office Assistant
- Medical Assistant-Admin./Clinical
- Medical Assistant - Front/Back
- Medical Assistant - Review
- Medical Insurance Billing
- Medical Records Specialist
- Medical Terminology
- Office Oper.-Clerical/Computers
- Office Support Specialist
- Principles of Real Estate
- Small Business Applications
- Teacher Aide

CLUSTER C - HUMANITARIAN - Related Occupations

- Athletic Trainer
- Case Worker
- Child Care Attendant
- Clergy Member
- Clinical Psychologist
- Counselor
- Dean of Students
- Dental Hygienist
- Dialysis Technician
- EKG Monitor Technician
- Emergency Medical Tech.
- Home Health Aide
- Human Services Occup.
- Medical Occupations
- Nurse Aide
- Nurse - Vocational
- Occupational Therapist
- Optometric Assistant
- Parole Officer
- Physical Therapist
- Physician Assistant
- Psychiatric Aide
- Psychologist
- Radiologic Technologist
- Recreation Therapist
- Residence Counselor
- Respiratory Therapist
- Social Worker
- Surgical Technician
- Teacher, Special Ed.

Related ROP Courses

- American Sign Language
- Child Care Occupations
- Dental Assistant: Fundamentals
- EKG Monitor Technician
- Emergency First Responder
- Health Careers: Introduction
- Hospital Careers: Intro.
- Hospital Health Careers
- Medical Asst. & Review (f&b)
- Medical Terminology
- Nurse Assistant, CNA, Acute
- Nursing Careers - Intro.
- Nursing - Vocational - Intro.
- Personal Fitness Trainer
- Pharmacy Technician
- Phlebotomy Technician
- Physical Therapy Aide
- Sports Therapy and Fitness
- Teacher Aide

CLUSTER D - INDUSTRIAL - Related Occupations

- Aircraft Assembler
- Aircraft Mechanic
- Baker
- Bindery Worker
- Brake Drum Lathe Oper.
- Casting-Machine Oper.
- Chemical Mixer
- Chem. Waste Treat. Oper.
- Control Panel Operator
- Cook
- Electronics Assembler
- Fiberglass Machine Operator
- Forklift Truck Operator
- Furniture Assembler
- Injection Molding
- Inspection Supervisor
- Machine Set-up Mechanic
- Moldmaking & Injection Molding
- Numerical Control Machine
- Numerical Lathe Operator
- Precision Lens Grinder
- Printer
- Quality Control Inspector
- Radial Arm Saw Operator
- Screw-Machine Operator
- Sewing Machine Operator
- Tool Grinder
- Veneer Lathe Operator
- Waste Treatment Plant Operator
- Welding Machine Operator

Related ROP Courses

- Bakery Occupations
- Furniture & Cabinet Manu./Fin.
- Computer Aided Drafting/Design
- Electrical Repair - Fund.
- Graphic Communications
- Machine Embroidery
- Motorcycle Maintenance
- Painting Occupations
- Railroad Careers
- Restaurant Occupations
- Warehouse/Distributive Occup.
- Woodworking Occupations
- Website Design
- Welding -- Cert. & Tech.

CLUSTER E - LEADING/INFLUENCING - Related Occupations

- Accountant
- Anthropologist
- Appraiser
- Arbitrator
- Archaeologist
- Camp Director
- Career Guidance Tech.
- City Planning Aide
- Claim Adjuster
- Credit Analyst
- Fashion Coordinator
- Fire Inspector
- Home Economist
- Hospitality Occupations
- Hotel Manager
- Human Services Occup.
- Income Tax Preparer
- Job Analyst
- Lawyer
- Librarian/Aide
- Newspaper Editor
- Paralegal Assistant
- Programmer
- Psychologist
- Real Estate Agent
- Safety Inspector
- Security Officer
- Sociologist
- Systems Analyst
- Teacher
- Urban Planner

Related ROP Courses

- Business Technology Lab
- Careers in Education
- Computer Network Mgmt.
- Desktop Publishing
- Entrepreneurship
- Financial Services Occup.
- Health Careers: Introduction
- Office Operations: Clerical
- Office Operations: Computer
- Principles of Real Estate
- Small Business Mgmt./Appli.
- Teacher Aide

CLUSTER F - MECHANICAL - Related Occupations

- Aeronautical Engineer
- Architect
- Auto Mechanic
- Bricklayer/Masonry
- Building Inspector/Maintenance
- Carpenter
- Civil Engineer
- Design Engineer
- Electronics Technician/Digital
- Facilities Planner
- Laser Technician
- Machinist
- Metal Fabricator
- Machinist & Numerical Control
- Office Machine Servicer
- Offset Press Operator
- Pilot/Aviation Occupations
- Pipe Fitter
- Prosthetics Technician
- Quality Control Engineer
- Safety Engineer
- Sound/Video Technician
- Surveyor
- Truck Driver

Related ROP Courses

- A+ Certification
- Auto Collision Repair
- Auto Engine Performance
- Auto Maintenance/Service
- Automotive Fundamentals
- Automotive Systems/Tech.
- Aviation Occupations
- Computer Aided Drafting
- Construction Trades
- Custodial Occupations
- Diesel Technology
- Digital Design
- Digital Electronics
- Electrical Repair: Fund.
- Furniture/Cabinet Manuf/Finish.
- Graphic Communications
- Motorcycle Maintenance
- NATEF-Cert. Sys.-Engine Perf.
- NATEF-Cert. Sys.-Align/Brakes
- Robotics
- Silkscreening
- Stagecraft Const. /Design
- Welding Cert./Technology

CLUSTER G - PERSONAL SERVICES - Related Occupations

- Automobile Rental Clerk
- Bus Driver
- Camp Counselor
- Cashier
- Catering
- Chauffeur
- Cosmetologist
- Counter Attendant
- Customer Service Clerk
- Driving Instructor
- Equipment Rental Clerk
- Flight Attendant
- Food Concession Manager
- Gambling Dealer
- Game Attendant
- Guide
- Hospitality Occupations
- Host/Hostess
- Manicurist
- Massage Therapist
- Newspaper Carrier
- Personal Fitness Trainer
- Recreation Leader
- Sales Clerk
- Ski Tow Operator
- Social Director
- Taxi Driver
- Waiter/Waitress
- Weight Reduction Spec.

Related ROP Courses

- Cosmetology
- Esthetician
- Manicuring - Nail Care
- Personal Fitness Trainer
- Physical Therapy Aide
- Recreation Occupations
- Restaurant Occupations

CLUSTER H - PHYSICAL PERFORMING - Related Occupations

- Agent
- Audio/Visual Productions
- Broadcasting Occupations
- Coach
- Professional Athlete
- Recreation Occupations
- Scout
- Sports Announcer
- Sports Instructor
- Stunt Performer
- Umpire

Related ROP Courses

- Personal Fitness Trainer
- Radio Broadcasting Occupations
- Sports Therapy & Fitness
- Stagecraft Construction/Design
- TV & Video Production

CLUSTER I - PLANT AND ANIMAL CARE – Related Occupations

- Animal Breeder
- Animal Caretaker
- Animal Health Care
- Aquaculture
- Cemetery Worker
- Dog Groomer
- Environmental Technology
- Farmer
- Field Inspector
- Fish Hatchery Worker
- Forester
- Forester Aide
- Forest Fire Fighter
- Game Preserve Manager
- Groundskeeper
- Horseshoer
- Horse Trainer
- Horticultural Worker
- Hydro-Sprayer Operator
- Landscape Contractor
- Landscape Gardener
- Livestock Rancher
- Logger
- Plant/Greenhouse Tech.
- Plant Propagator
- Skiff Operator
- Stock Ranch Supervisor
- Tree Surgeon
- Veterinarian
- Wildlife Control Agent

Related ROP Courses

- Floral Design & Sales
- Geographic Info. Systems
- Landscape Maint./Design
- Veterinary Assistant
- Wildland Firefighting:Fund.

CLUSTER J - PROTECTIVE – Related Occupations

- Airline Security Rep.
- Armored Car Guard
- Bailiff
- Bodyguard
- Correction Officer
- Detective
- Dispatcher
- Firefighter
- Fire Inspector
- Fire Marshall
- Fish & Game Warden
- Immigration Officer
- Internal Security Manager
- Lifeguard
- Park Ranger
- Police Officer
- Private Investigator
- Security Guard
- Wildlife Agent

Related ROP Courses

- Advanced Law Enforcement
- Fire Technology
- Geographic Info. Systems
- Law Enforcement: Fundamentals
- Wildland Firefighting: Fundamentals

CLUSTER K - SALES – Related Occupations

- Auctioneer
- Broker
- Buyer
- Communications Consult.
- Demonstrator
- Estate Planner
- Fashion Merchandising
- Group Sales Rep.
- Hospitality Occupations
- Leasing Agent
- Route Salesperson
- Sales Agent
- Sales and Merchandising
- Sales Clerk
- Sales Representative
- Sales Route Driver
- Sporting Goods Sales
- Telephone Solicitor
- Travel Agent
- Vendor
- Wedding Consultant

Related ROP Courses

- Auto Parts Specialist
- Business Technology Lab
- Careers in Marketing/Retail Sales
- Customer Service Occupations
- Desktop Publishing
- Entrepreneurship
- Financial Services Occu.
- Floral Design & Sales
- Graphic Communications
- Office Operations: Clerical
- Principles of Real Estate
- Product Prep. & Assembly
- Silk Screening
- Small Business Appl.

CLUSTER L - SCIENTIFIC– Related Occupations

- Agronomist
- Anesthesiologist
- Animal Health Care
- Audiologist
- Biologist
- Biomedical Engineering
- Biotechnology
- Cardiologist
- Chemist
- Chiropractor
- Computer Forensics
- Coroner
- Dentist
- Dermatologist
- Ecologist
- Environmental Technology
- Fingerprint Classifier
- Food Technologist
- Hydrologist
- Laboratory Technician
- Medical Technologist
- Meteorologist
- Neurologist
- Ophthalmologist
- Orthopedic Technician
- Pathologist
- Pharmacist
- Seismologist
- Soil Scientist
- Speech Pathologist
- Ultrasound Technologist
- Veterinarian
- Zoologist

Related ROP Courses

- Dental Assistant - Fund./Regis.
- Emergency First Responder
- Health Careers: Introduction
- Hospital Careers: Introduction
- Hospital Health Careers
- Medical Assistant-Back/Front
- Medical Assistant Review
- Medical Terminology
- Nurse Assistant, Cert./Acute
- Pharmacy Technician
- Phlebotomy Technician
- Sports Therapy & Fitness

Robin Rask

Name: _____   DATE: _____

Research An Occupation

Occupational Title: _____

The O-Net Dictionary of Occupations _____
You can share this job with the class

Nature of the work: *List some of the tasks/job skills a person must perform in this job.*

_____   _____

_____   _____

Training, High School/GED, other qualifications & advancement: *Describe in one or two sentences.*

_____

_____

_____

Working Conditions: *Describe in one or two sentences.*

_____

_____

_____

Job Outlook: *What is the expected growth and opportunities?*

_____

_____

Earnings: *What are the average earnings?* _____   *annually/monthly/hourly*
(circle one)

Related Careers: *List three alternative careers that require similar skills.*

_____   _____   _____

Where did you find this information? OOH, Computer, O-net, Bridges, Professional Organizations.

_____

What do you like or dislike about this occupation?

_____

_____

_____

8

Dressing for a Successful Interview

A series of TV ads have used the slogan "Image is everything." In job interviews, image is not everything, but it is important, and the way you dress contributes to that image. Creating that right appearance is one of the many ways you can prepare for the interview and when applying for a job.

Winning Appearance

Neat and clean

Matching colors

In good taste

Nothing trendy

Nothing flashy

How To Dress For Your Job Search

Appropriate Attire

Men	Women
➢ dress shirt (button down)	➢ skirt
➢ pressed slacks	➢ blouse
➢ dress shoes	➢ dress
➢ dark socks	➢ suit (dark color)
➢ tie (if appropriate)	➢ blazer or jacket
➢ sport coat	➢ nylons (skin tones)
➢ suit (professional)	➢ dress shoes (pumps, low heels)
➢ hair cut	➢ simple jewelry
➢ fresh shaven	➢ pantsuit (professional)
➢ nails (clean and cut)	➢ hair color check
➢ watch	➢ nail polish check
	➢ watch

Inappropriate Attire

➢ blue jeans	➢ miniskirts or shorts
➢ t-shirts	➢ T-shirts
➢ shorts	➢ tight dresses or see-through clothing
➢ tennis shoes	➢ blue jeans
➢ gym/exercise clothes	➢ gym/exercise clothes
➢ heavy cologne or aftershave	➢ heavy makeup/perfume
➢ Earrings	➢ bright nail polish
➢ Visible tattoos or facial piercings	➢ visible tattoos or facial piercings

Sources of Employment

Sources of employment are plentiful. Here are several:

- apprenticeship programs
- Avon or business directories
- California Conservation Corps (CCC)
- canvassing
- chambers of commerce
- civil service announcements
- communications media
- employment development departments
- industrial parks
- job bulletin boards
- Job Corps
- job fairs
- local newspapers
- manufacturers or distributors of special equipment used at work
- military services
- newspaper advertisements
- private employment agencies
- professional and business associations
- radio, TV, newspapers, and magazine stories of new or expanding companies or areas
- ROP training
- school placement services
- suppliers, customers, and competitors of prior employers
- teachers, religious advisers, insurance agents, creditors, bankers
- trade associations and publications
- unions and friends, relatives, and neighbors
- volunteer
- websites

A good percentage of jobs are filled through networking.

MASTER APPLICATION
PLEASE PRINT CLEARLY AND ANSWER ALL QUESTIONS FULLY

Date of Application:_____

NAME_____
            LAST   FIRST   MIDDLE

ADDRESS_____

CITY_____STATE_____ZIP_____PHONE(_____)_____

SOCIAL SECURITY NUMBER_____-_____-_____   (Optional)

Do you have a Class C (Regular) Driver's License? ☐ Yes ☐ No   California ID? ☐ Yes ☐ No

Schedule Desired: ☐ Full Time ☐ Part Time ☐ Seasonal   Date Available for work:_____

Shift Desired: ☐ Day ☐ Evenings ☐ Any Hours   Salary Expected: $_____

		Sunday	Monday	Tuesday	Wednesday	Thursday	Friday	Saturday
Available	Day							
Hours	Evening							

List activities or commitments that may interfere with attendance requirements:_____
_____

POSITION APPLYING FOR:_____ Are you 18 years old or older? ☐ Yes ☐ No

Do you have any relatives employed by this company? ☐ Yes ☐ No

Are you eligible/authorized to work in the United States? ☐ Yes ☐ No

WORK HISTORY: List ALL employment beginning with the most recent. Include military, voluntary and unpaid work experience.

Company	Period of Employment & Salary	Title & Description
Supervisor	From: To:	
Phone ( )	Start:$ End:$	
Address		
City/State/Zip		
Reason for Leaving		
Company	Period of Employment & Salary	Title & Description
Supervisor	From: To:	
Phone ( )	Start:$ End:$	
Address		
City/State/Zip		
Reason for Leaving		
Company	Period of Employment & Salary	Title & Description
Supervisor	From: To:	
Phone ( )	Start:$ End:$	
Address		
City/State/Zip		
Reason for Leaving		
Company	Period of Employment & Salary	Title & Description
Supervisor	From: To:	
Phone ( )	Start:$ End:$	
Address		
City/State/Zip		
Reason for Leaving		

(OVER PLEASE)

Company	Period of Employment & Salary	Title & Description
Supervisor	From: To:	
Phone ( )	Start:$ End:$	
Address		
City/State/Zip		
Reason for Leaving		
Company	Period of Employment & Salary	Title & Description
Supervisor	From: To:	
Phone ( )	Start:$ End:$	
Address		
City/State/Zip		
Reason for Leaving		

What method of transportation will you use?_____

Can you speak any foreign languages?_____

Have you ever been convicted of a felony?   ☐ Yes   ☐ No   If yes, please explain_____

_____

A conviction may not neccesarily bar you from employment.
Each conviction will be judged on its own merits with respect to time, circumstances and seriousness.

Can you pass a drug test **TODAY**?   ☐ Yes   ☐ No   If no, Please explain:_____

_____

Describe any special training or skills you have:_____

_____

Additional Information for Placement Consideration_____

_____

Education

	School Name	Location	Graduate	Degree	Major/Minor	G.P.A.
High School						
College						
Business/Tech						
Other / ROP						

References

Name	Address, City, State & Phone	Business	Years Known

I certify that all the information submitted by me on this application is true and complete to the best of my knowledge.

Date_____   Signature_____

How to Find a Job

Many people are out of work for a variety of reasons. There are people who want to work and people who do not. Some people cannot find jobs because they don't know how or they do not have the tools they need. Some people hold signs on street corners begging for money, and some of them make nine to fifteen dollars per hour. The good news is if you want to work, the jobs are plentiful. As long as Earth remains, there will always be jobs.

Some companies always accept applications, and some hire constantly. We have to learn to think outside the box. Think about the types of products and services we need and are always in demand, such as food, clothing, medicine, automotive services, law enforcement, firefighting, retail, distribution, bridge building, electricians, plumbers, teachers, counselors, computer techs, hair stylists, manicurists—the list is endless.

Sometimes we have to go back to school or gain additional training. In addition, there are always seasonal hires, many of which turn into part-time or full-time jobs. There is always someone hiring!

Applications

Tangible Applications

For the few companies that still accept tangible applications, take a sample application with all your information written out and transfer the information to the company's application. It is important to know the names of your past employers, their addresses and phone numbers, when you started, when you left, and other relevant facts. Keeping a sample copy of an application in your portfolio or a file is vital. When you submit your application in person, make sure to include a copy of your résumé. This guide includes a sample application, or you can pick one up from a business.

Employers look to make sure the application is completely filled out and neat. Make sure to use a black or blue ink pen. If something does not apply to you, make sure to write "N/A," put a dash, or write "None." Do not leave anything blank. Employers then look for your experience and availability. When an application asks for salary desired, you can write "open," "entry-level," or "negotiable."

Online Applications

You may be able to fill out an online application at a computer desk at a business. The majority of the time, you can do it from home. Either way, you will need to have your sample application next to you to fill out an online application. You will also need your social security number. A test almost always follows an online application, and it is usually timed. This guide includes a sample test to give you an idea of what to expect. Some are easy; others are very challenging.

Following up with the employer is vital after completing the online application so you can inquire if you passed, are being considered for the job, or to find out what the next step might be.

Some high school graduates cannot fill out online applications and take the tests without assistance. This deters some of them from seeking employment. How will algebra or all the testing help them obtain a job if they cannot fill out an application tangibly or online? Schools could take them to the computer lab and allow them to apply online and take the tests so they know what to expect. For those who are doing this, *thank you!* Our education process needs to change. There are also not enough consequences for cell phones. There should be no tolerance for them in the classroom.

On a personal note, I have to say that finding a job was much easier before we had to fill out applications online and take those silly tests. It is a shame because many of us may be qualified for the job, but because we did not pass the online test, we aren't considered for employment. There is a thirty-to ninety-day waiting period before you can take the test again, depending on the company. With some companies, the wait is six months.

Who knows what lies ahead? Maybe they will consider going back to old school and what works.

Video Résumés

Some employers and companies, including colleges, may want you to create a video of yourself summarizing your skills and attributes. If that is the case, make sure to dress to impress and have an appropriate background setting without any noise. Then display your professionalism as you would in person.

Skype Interviews

Prepare as you would for a video résumé. You need to conduct yourself as you would in person. It is still a face-to-face interview, except that you are looking at each other on a computer screen. Skype interviews are common, especially when you are applying for jobs outside your area or state.

ID Cards

My advice for young folks looking for work is to make sure you have an ID card from the DMV. Your school ID card will no longer be valid when you go to work, so you need to apply for an ID as soon as you know you may be going to work or at least before you leave high school. This guide includes information on how to apply for your ID card with the DMV.

Social Security Cards

Most students do not sign their social security cards. This can be dangerous and leave you open to identity theft. As soon as you receive your social security card, sign it, make a copy of it, and put it somewhere safe. Also memorize the number so you will never forget it. That is what we had to do back in the day. Today most students don't memorize their socials and sometimes not even their address or phone numbers. This all needs to start at home.

Work Permits

If you are in still in school and under the age of eighteen, you will need a work permit to work. Check with your school to obtain the work permit application. Fill out your part, have a parent sign it, and then take it to the job site and have the employer fill out his or her part. Then take it back to your school; they will type up the actual work permit that will go back to the work site when you start working.

W-4 Forms

It is amazing how many students and young folks do not know about this form and how to fill it out. Everyone hired by an employer has to fill out the W-4 and I-9 form for employment. They are two very simple forms asking for your personal information and signature. One major issue on the I-9 form is that the month, day, and year have to be exactly written out as mm/dd/yyyy—07/17/2020 is a correct example. This is recommended by the Department of Homeland Security. The same applies to birth dates. Several personnel managers have told me that this is a challenge because you cannot whiteout the date. Sometimes they cross a line through it and initial it. Many write the date 7/17/20 or 7-20-20. These are both incorrect. This is another great activity to teach in the classroom.

What most young folks do not understand on the W-4 is the withholding allowance and that it is subject to change when you get married and have children. You need to know that this affects your income tax return. Schools and parents should be teaching this. It would be a great lesson to teach in the classroom to prepare students to go to work. For those of you who are, *thank you!* Instead of all the testing, we need to prepare our students for the future and going to work. Many are not prepared. This is a tragedy. I know because I deal with this constantly.

Social Media

According to *Career Builder*, in 2016, some 43 percent of hiring managers now use social media to screen potential candidates. At this time, LinkedIn seems to be the largest professional network on the Internet. In addition, there are thirty-nine million students and graduates on LinkedIn, which means that will continue to grow. Therefore, I highly suggest that you always conduct yourself professionally. Be careful with your social media contacts. You should consider making your public profile visible to no one or you open yourself up to hackers. Anything you put on the Internet is out there for everyone to see and often forever. Always remember that!

Robin's Simple Recipe

Robin's Simple Recipe is like going on a diet: if you follow it, you will obtain a job. The key is persistence and *always following up*. Make sure you dress to impress, have a résumé and sample application, and be able to sell yourself. In other words, be prepared to answer questions about yourself and your skills. There are occasions when applicants apply for a job in person and they can be interviewed on the spot. Therefore, display enthusiasm!

The candidate (you) should begin the search process by submitting applications to at least ten job sites. You should take your application to the manager and introduce yourself. Always smile and shake hands. Say, "Hello, I'm (your name). I stopped by to provide you with a copy of my application and résumé. I want you to know I am really interested in working here." The rest is up to the employer. When you leave a job site, write down where you visited, who you saw, and what was said. Keep a log sheet of where you went so you will be able to follow up. Every week or two, go back to those places, ask for the manager, reintroduce yourself, and let the manager know you are still interested in working there. If you had to complete an application online, still follow up in person whenever possible. Increasing the number of places you apply and following up will assist you in becoming hired sooner rather than later.

Often the best time to find a job is when you have one. You can always accept a job and then continue to search for the one you are truly interested in during the time you are not contracted to work. You should not become discouraged; expect to hear some no's and stay positive. Consistency is the key to victory! There are many employment agencies available to assist people having difficulties in finding a job as well.

Answering Machines

If you are looking for a job, it is important to make sure you have a professional outgoing message on all of your phones. For example: "Hi! You have reached Robin. Sorry I am not available to take your call right now, but please leave a message, and I will return your call as soon as possible." We have all heard way too many things that are not acceptable. Employers could call you and, because of your outgoing voice mail, they may just hang up. And they have!

Robin's One-Page Recipe for Finding a Job
(Follow this and/or copy)

Apply where you want to work and continue to go back to let them know you are interested in working there. Always dress to interview when you apply for a job and always go alone. Fill out your application neatly and completely; if something does not apply to you, write "N/A." Always use black or blue pen and take whiteout with you or an erasable pen. You may attach a résumé to your application or make sure to bring one to your meeting and interview.

When you turn in your application, ask for the manager so you can introduce yourself. Shake his or her hand, smile, and show enthusiasm. Say, "Nice to meet you. I just wanted to give you my application and let you know that I am interested in working here." That is all you have to say. When you leave, write down where you visited, the date, the manager's name, and what he or she said. Keep a log sheet of everywhere you go. When you go back to do your weekly or biweekly follow up, you will know who to ask for. If they tell you to come back on a certain day or time, make sure that you do. If they tell you to call on Tuesday at 4:00 and you don't, that tells the employer that you do not want the job.

The more places you apply and follow up on, the sooner you will get hired. Many times you will be interviewed on the spot, so be prepared. The number one question asked in interviews is "Can you tell me about yourself?" Therefore, you need to be ready to talk about yourself. Let them know what your strengths are, what kind of person you are, and how you can fit in with the company. Work on your personal attributes; we all have them. Example: Look in the mirror every morning and start talking to yourself. Say whatever applies to you, such as, "I am a team player, organized, creative, a fast learner, and responsible, always take initiative, and have great time-management skills." Making personal confessions of your attributes will make you a more positive person and you will be able to sell yourself better in an interview. It will also help to have a portfolio to bring with you to your interview. Some of the things to put in your portfolio are the following:

résumé, references, and recommendation letters

certificates, awards, report cards, transcripts, vocational training, internships, ROP classes, and pictures of accomplishments

outside activities, clubs, community service, etc.

You don't have a second chance to make a good first impression!

Make sure you stay persistent and follow up! If you are looking for a job and can't find one, you either don't know how to effectively search for a job or you are not motivated. Remember to network, use all your resources, and attend job fairs.

THERE IS SOMEONE HIRING EVERY DAY! GOOD LUCK!

Job Leads Log Sheet

Date	Employer Name & Address	Phone Number & Contact Person	Currently Hiring	Date Contacted	Comments/Notes
_____		Phone Number: Contact Person: Title:	____Yes ____ No When _____	Follow-up:	Application Submitted: ____ Yes____No When_____ Resume Submitted: ____ Yes____No When_____ Interview Scheduled: ____ Yes____No When_____
_____		Phone Number: Contact Person: Title:	____Yes ____ No When _____	Follow-up:	Application Submitted: ____ Yes ____ No When_____ Resume Submitted: ____ Yes ____ No When_____ Interview Scheduled: ____ Yes ____ No When_____
_____		Phone Number: Contact Person: Title:	____Yes ____ No When _____	Follow-up:	Application Submitted: ____ Yes ____ No When_____ Resume Submitted: ____ Yes ____ No When_____ Interview Scheduled: ____ Yes ____ No When_____
_____		Phone Number: Contact Person: Title:	____Yes ____ No When _____	Follow-up:	Application Submitted: ____ Yes ____ No When_____ Resume Submitted: ____Yes ____ No When_____ Interview Scheduled: ____ Yes ____ No When_____
_____		Phone Number: Contact Person: Title:	____Yes ____No When _____	Follow-up:	Application Submitted: ____ Yes ____ No When_____ Resume Submitted: ____Yes ____ No When_____ Interview Scheduled: ____ Yes ____ No When_____

1. How was (or is) your behavior in high school?
- O a. Never caused any trouble.
- O b. Occasionally caused minor problems.
- O c. Often caused problems.
- O d. Was a real trouble maker.
- O e. Didn't attend high school.

2. How was (or is) your attendance in school?
- O a. Missed less than a day each year.
- O b. Missed one to four days a year.
- O c. Missed five to ten days a year.
- O d. Missed 11-15 days a year.
- O e. Missed more than 15 days a year.

3. How well do you do at most things you try?
- O a. You always succeed and do better than most people.
- O b. You do most things as well as other people do.
- O c. You usually get things done, but not as well as you want.
- O d. You often try to do too much and have to give up.
- O e. You don't try to do many things.

4. If you are hired for this job, what do you think are your chances of becoming an excellent employee?
- O a. Certain to become excellent.
- O b. Probably become excellent.
- O c. Fifty-fifty chance to become excellent.
- O d. Probably will not become excellent.
- O e. Don't know

5. If you are hired for this job, how long do you think you will keep it?
- O a. A few weeks.
- O b. 1 or 2 months
- O c. 3 or 4 months
- O d. 5 or 6 months
- O e. More than 6 months

6. What kind of employee do you believe is best – one who:
- O a. Comes up with a lot of good ideas to improve the job.
- O b. Is always friendly to other employees.
- O c. Follows every company rule
- O d. Is hardly ever absent.
- O e. Starts work without being told to.

7. Which kind of employee do you believe is poorest – one who:
- O a. Refuses to work a fair share of overtime.
- O b. Skips work and doesn't call in.
- O c. Is a few minutes late almost every day.
- O d. Takes home some small company property.
- O e. Works much slower than others on the job.

8. How many times in your life have you known someone who has taken something from a car without permission?
- O a. Never
- O b. Once or twice
- O c. From 3 to 6 times
- O d. from 7 to 10 times
- O e. More than 10 times.

9. How often have you owned merchandise that somebody else may have stolen?
- O a. Never
- O b. Once or twice.
- O c. From 3 to 6 times.
- O d. From 7 to 10 times.
- O e. More than 10 times.

10. How many times in your life have you gotten into physical fights?
- O a. Never
- O b. Once or twice.
- O c. Between 3 and 6 times.
- O d. Between 7 and 10 times.
- O e. More than 10 times.

11. How many times in your life have your been praised by your teachers of bosses?
- O a. Never
- O b. Once or twice.
- O c. Between 3 and 6 times
- O d. Between 7 and 10 times.
- O e. More than 10 times

1.		2.	
○	a. Generous	○	a. Tolerant
○	b. Orderly	○	b. Responsible
○	c. Sincere	○	c. Active

3.		4.	
○	a. Helpful	○	a. Serious
○	b. Steady	○	b. Systematic
○	c. Creative	○	c. Informal

5.		6.	
○	a. Logical	○	a. Reliable
○	b. Patient	○	b. Energetic
○	c. Hardworking	○	c. Pleasant

7.		8.	
○	a. Good natured	○	a. Persistent
○	b. Stable	○	b. Brave
○	c. Fair minded	○	c. Clear thinking

9.		10.	
○	a. Curious	○	a. Eager
○	b. Conforming	○	b. Skillful
○	c. Persuasive	○	c. Honest

	T	F			T	F	
1.			When you make a mistake, it's natural for you to try to cover it up.	2.			You are very cautious in most things you do.
3.			Taking orders is part of every job.	4.			You have an excellent memory for details.
5.			You have never used a telephone or watched TV.	6.			You are street smart.
7.			You feel disgusted with the law when a criminal gets off because of some legal technicality.	8.			Your are known as a very careful person.
9.			Everyone at some time in their adult life has stolen something.	10.			In school or on a job, you have gotten into trouble for fooling around.
11.			Your social life makes it hard for you to work evenings.	12.			You are completely optimistic about your future.
13.			You would not quit a job unless you had another lined up.	14.			You go by the saying "Don't get mad – get even"
15.			Eating properly can be important to our health.	16.			There have been times when you have had too much alcohol to drink.
17.			The members of your family have gotten along well together.	18.			Once in a while you feel a little lazy.
19.			You would (or do) enjoy dangerous activities like sky diving or race car driving.	20.			You work steady and hard at whatever you undertake.
21.			When you were growing up, you had a lot of disagreements with your parents.	22.			Stores are against shoplifting and theft.
23.			You like to create excitement no matter what situation you are in.	24.			During your youth, your family often disapprove of your choices.
25.			Becoming successful is mostly a matter of being in the right place at the right time.	26.			You love to take chances.
27.			Your home life has been happy and pleasant.	28.			You definitely are not a thrill seeker.
29.			Travel in this country is slower now than 100 years ago.	30.			You have never hurt someone's feelings.
31			You feel embarrassed when someone else makes a dumb mistake.	32.			You would never talk back to a boss or a teacher.
33.			It's no use doing things for other people – they never pay you back.	34.			You like to do things that shock people.
35.			Computers now do a lot of what people used to do by hand.	36.			It is important to have friends in the right places to get you out of trouble.
37.			You freely admit your mistakes.	38.			You have some bad habits that you have tried to break but just haven't been able to.
39.			You tend to make quick decisions based on your first reaction to a situation.	40.			You cannot count past 50.
41.			Most places don't care much if employees take a few things home with them from work.	42.			You almost always do more than is required in your work or school projects.
43.			There should be a lot more police to control the high crime rate.	44.			It doesn't matter if your friends get into trouble as long as it doesn't involve you.
45.			It is hard for you to put up with someone else's stupid mistakes.	46.			You have never been fired from a job.
47.			You demand a lot, sometimes too much, from yourself.	48.			Sometimes you feel uneasy all day for no reason.
49.			If you could live your life over again, you would certainly do things differently next time.	50.			Most bosses don't care if their employees always come late to work.

Online Applications Tests

As many of you know most employers expect you to fill out the job application online now. And most of them have assessment tests afterwards. There are several scenarios of questions. Some are simple and others more complicated. They basically want to know what type of characteristic traits you have.

Many of the questions have a section where they ask different ways on agreeing or disagreeing with the questions. Bottom line, you need to strongly agree that it is right or strongly disagree that it is wrong. You may not agree with some of the options. However, you do need to be consistent with your answers. Some of the assessment includes math, problem solving and common sense. Some of the questions you really have to think about how you will respond. Sometimes there is more than one answer but you can only select one. I suggest you keep a calculator near you and consider having someone sit with you to assist in answering the questions.

HERE ARE SOME EXAMPLES:

1. **It is ok to have a drink before you come to work?**

A. **Strongly agree**

B. **Somewhat agree**

C. **Slightly agree**

D. **Strongly disagree**

E. **Somewhat disagree**

F. **Slightly disagree**

Answer: D

2. **How often do you get angry?**

A. **I never get angry**

B. **I rarely get angry**

C. **I sometimes get angry**

D. **I often get angry**

Answer: A

Then again, it could be rarely or sometimes depending on you.

3. **I have difficulties building relationships.**

A. **Definetly true**

B. **Somewhat true**

C. **I don't know**

D. **Somewhat false**

E. **Definetly false**

Answer: E

Some people do have challenges building relationships.

4. **You are assisting a customer who is hard to understand, what would you do?**

A. **Ask a supervisor to take care of the customer**

B. **Listen to the customer carefully and make the best guess on what was said?**

C. **Ask the customer to wait while you find someone who can understand?**

D. **Ask the customer to come back later when there is someone else to assist?**

E. **Apologize for not understanding and ask the customer to speak slower so you can understand?**

Answer: E

Sometimes you cannot help and need to seek additional help.

5.   How often do people come to you for suggestions or advise?

A. **Always**

B. **Frequently**

C. **Occasionaly**

D. **Seldom**

E. **Never**

Answer: A

With me it is B and C, because I am not in management.

6.   How do you typically handle stress on the job or at school?

A. **I speed up so I can handle the extra I work slower but concentrate more**

B. **I rely on others more when I am under stress**

C. **Stress does not influence how I approach my work**

D. **I work slower but concentrate more**

Answer: C

Sometimes for me it is A.

7.   My friends and family tell me that I am too focused on details.

A. **Definetly True**

B. **More True than False**

C. **More False than True**

D. **Definetly False**

Answer: A

On a personal note, I have had students who were trained for two hundred hours in a retail store under a work program who took the assessment and failed. How can this be fair when they are already doing the job? I have been told by Human Resource departments that many of them could not pass the tests. As some of us say, "It is what it is."

Answer: Someone needs to change this!

Informational Interviews

One of the best ways to find out about a job or a career area in which you are interested in, is to talk to people who are actually doing the job or to those who hire those individuals. Informational interviewing is a foot in the door and an extremely effective tool for finding a job and/or deciding what you want and do not want to do. You could actually make a career out of conducting informational interviews.

An informational interview is not applying for a job; it is strictly obtaining information about a specific job or career. Therefore, it is not as nerve-racking. Conducting an informational interview can be synonymous with writing a story as a journalist. In other words, you are the one asking the questions. This can be fun and informative at the same time. It may also help increase your self-confidence as you gain additional knowledge in a particular field. I tell my applicants this is a golden method, but most people do not want to put the time and effort into conducting informational interviews. It has been said, "Those who search the most, find the most." God says the same thing in the Bible, "Seek and you shall find."

Conducting Your Informational Interview

Select a job you would like or a career you want to pursue. You can do this with any company you want. Let's say you want to work for Best Buy. Pick up the phone, call Best Buy, and ask for the manager's name. Thank them and hang up the phone. Now write down some questions about what you may want to know about Best Buy and how to obtain a job there. Your intent will now be to set up a meeting to find out about the company. When you are ready, call Best Buy again and ask for the manager by name. When the manager comes to the phone, say, "Hi, Mr. Smith. My name is Robin Rask. I am conducting research on your company and was wondering if I could schedule an informational interview with you at your earliest convenience." Mr. Smith might say yes, and then you set up a time and day.

Keep in mind that you are not going on a job interview. You are only gathering information. However, in the back of your mind, you want to work for Best Buy, but you cannot tell them that. Ask questions that will help you find out what the employer is looking for, what experience is needed, and how often they hire. You need to come up with about five to six questions. This will help you to determine if you want to work there or not.

Here are some questions you could ask:

- What are the different types of positions you have and what are the duties?
- How often do you hire?
- What is your method of hiring?
- What do you look for in an applicant?
- What is an entry-level position here?
- What is your entry-level salary?
- What are your expectations of the applicants you hire?
- What is the dress code?
- Does your company offer promotions and/or benefits?
- What type of training do you provide?

These are just some examples. But always ask some things about the company first and then ask those questions that would benefit you. You should write your questions out on a tablet and leave room to write down the manager's responses. Then take your tablet to the meeting. If you have difficulty with writing and listening at the same time, take a tape recorder with you. At the meeting, make sure to ask the employer if it is okay to record the conversation.

When you go to the informational interview, it is extremely important that you dress professionally. Always dress to impress! You want to make a good first impression just as you would on an actual job interview. Make sure to arrive on time. When you walk in, ask for Mr. Smith. When Mr. Smith comes out, shake his hand, and greet him by saying, "Hello, Mr. Smith. I am Robin. I spoke with you on the phone about meeting with you today to discuss your company." Sometimes employers will forget that they scheduled that kind of meeting with you. Chances are you will then go into his office or somewhere else within the company.

Before you begin asking questions, you may want to break the ice by making a comment. That is up to you. You may start off by saying, "Great office," or "Looks like you are busy here today." Once you sit down, one of the first questions you ask needs to be about the manager personally, such as, "How long have you been working for Best Buy?" or "Do you enjoy working here?" Then when the time is right, you can begin asking questions. The interview may take anywhere from fifteen minutes to an hour, depending on the employer's time. Please be considerate of his or her time and be patient with any interruptions.

At the end of the interview, make sure you thank the employer for his or her time. Shake his or her hand again and ask if he or she has a business card. You may also ask if he or she knows any other businesses you could interview. Everyone knows someone. There may be times when you conduct your interview and the employer may say, "It just so happens that we are hiring right now. Why don't you pick up an application on your way out or apply online?" Thank him or her and say that you just came today to gather some information about the company and are not prepared to fill out an application, but you would like to think about it.

Keep in mind your intent was to inquire information about the company, not apply for a job. If the employer insists that you take an application, please do so.

When you arrive home after your interview, place a thank-you card or letter in the mail to the employer, thanking him or her for his or her time. Then you can review the information gathered from the company and decide if you would like to work for the company. You can do this with as many companies as you want. The worst thing that can happen is that you are offered a job!

If you are interested in the job or company, go back and apply or apply online. The employer already knows you and will admire you for coming in on your own time to inquire about his business. When you return, ask for an application and fill it out. Then ask for Mr. Smith. When Mr. Smith comes out, greet him, shake his hand, and say, "After meeting with you the other day, I decided that I would like the opportunity to work for Best Buy. Here is my application and résumé." Or you can say, "I filled out my application online, and I wanted to give you a copy of my résumé and let you know that I am really interested in working here." The rest is in his hands.

This is a great way to think outside the box and obtain a job!

This is also an activity that may be used in the classroom. See the following worksheets I used for my ROP classes. The students read their informational interviews out loud to the class and were given fifty points. This also allowed other students to hear about different jobs and careers. We need to give our students better tools to help them become more prepared and successful!

Another Approach

The Informational Interview

(Copy and use as your guide)

The best way to find out about a job or career area in which you are interested is to talk to the people who are actually doing the job—or even better, talk to the person who hires those people. This method of employer contact, called the informational interview, can also be a very effective job-seeking method.

To arrange for an informational interview, call the personnel department of a company and ask to talk with the person who hires workers in the area of your interest. Ask if you can set up an appointment to come in and talk with him or her for about fifteen minutes at his or her convenience. Explain that you are thinking about going into that type of work someday and would like to know more about the work as well as what kind of training, experience, and personality characteristics the employer looks for.

Remember, you are seeking information, not interviewing for a job. You will be asking questions of the employer, so you should be prepared. You should dress appropriately and act somewhat businesslike, as you will want to leave a positive impression. Be courteous and sensitive to the cues of the employer.

Do not take up too much of the employer's time since he or she is doing you a favor by agreeing to talk with you. Most employers do not mind this type of request, and most feel flattered to have their advice sought.

When you have finished with your list of questions for the employer, thank him or her for the time. Do not offer a copy of your résumé. If the employer requests it, return with it at a later time. You do not want the employer to feel he or she was tricked into a job interview.

Sometimes, you may find out that you are already qualified for the job about which you are inquiring. An employer may request your résumé or suggest that you apply for a specific job. Employers sometimes suggest further contact and may even give you permission to use their name. These happenings would provide extra benefits to your main goal of seeking information although some experts have speculated that doing information interviews actually more than doubles your job-seeking success.

Always be courteous and try to make a good impression. You never know when you may encounter that employer again as you are applying for jobs or even when you are working on a job. Finally, be certain to send the employer a brief letter or card thanking him or her for taking the time to talk with you.

DREAM JOB INFORMATIONAL INTERVIEW WORKSHEET

Company's Name:_____   Date: _____

Interviewer's Name: _____   Phone No.: _____

Student's Name: _____

REQUIREMENT QUESTIONS

QUESTIONS & ANSWERS	Would I like this?		Could I do this?	
1. What are the job duties?	Yes	No	Yes	No
2. What are the training or educational requirements of the job?	Yes	No	Yes	No
3. What experience must people have to start here?	Yes	No	Yes	No
4. What are the physical demands of the job (lifting, standing, etc)?	Yes	No	Yes	No
5. What are the hours of the job?	Yes	No	Yes	No
6. What kinds of equipment (vehicles, machinery, computers, etc., must a worker be able to operate to do the job?	Yes	No	Yes	No
7. Are there other jobs in this field that might have fewer requirements?	Yes	No	Yes	No

WORK SKILLS QUESTIONS

QUESTIONS & ANSWERS

	Would I like this?		Could I do this?	
1. How important are speed and accuracy on this job?				
	Yes	No	Yes	No
2. What are the company's safety practices?				
	Yes	No	Yes	No
3. What is the daily routine of the job?				
	Yes	No	Yes	No
4. What are the reading, writing and math requirements of the job?				
	Yes	No	Yes	No

SOCIAL SKILLS QUESTIONS

QUESTIONS & ANSWERS

	Would I like this?		Could I do this?	
1. Do workers have contact with customers? If yes, what is the policy for customer interaction?				
	Yes	No	Yes	No
2. Does the company have a probation period?				
	Yes	No	Yes	No
3. Does the company have social activities?				
	Yes	No	Yes	No

PERSONAL SKILLS QUESTIONS

QUESTIONS & ANSWERS

	Would I like this?		Could I do this?	
1. What is the dress code?				
	Yes	No	Yes	No
2. What kind of personal traits must workers have to do this job?				
	Yes	No	Yes	No
3. What things must workers have (uniforms, lunch, special shoes, tools., etc.)?				
	Yes	No	Yes	No

COMPANY POLICY AND ATMOSPHERE QUESTIONS

QUESTIONS & ANSWERS

Questions & Answers	Would I like this?		Could I do this?	
1. How often do people get hired?	Yes	No	Yes	No
2. How does the company hire – newspaper, agencies, walk-ins, referrals, EDD?	Yes	No	Yes	No
3. What is the entry level wage for this job?	Yes	No	Yes	No
4. What benefits can workers at this site receive?	Yes	No	Yes	No
5. What kind of training do workers receive?	Yes	No	Yes	No
6. Are workers closely supervised?	Yes	No	Yes	No
7. How are workers evaluated?	Yes	No	Yes	No
8. Is there a possibility of promotion?	Yes	No	Yes	No

SUMMARY

Would I like this job?   YES   NO
(Consider the number of times you chose "Yes" and "No" in the "Would I like this?" column.)

Why or why not?

Could I do this job?   YES   NO
(Consider the number of times you chose "Yes" and "No" in the "Could I do this" column.

Why or why not?

Additional questions or comments:

Job Shadowing

Job shadowing allows people the opportunity to learn what another person actually does in a job that is of interest to them. When a person job shadows in the workplace, he or she observes firsthand the skills and knowledge required to be successful on the job. This is a great time to take notes, observe, and ask questions.

The experience can stimulate one's interest in an industry or specific occupation. Or in some cases, it may steer him or her away from something in which he or she has little or no interest.

Setting up a job shadow is similar to conducting an informational interview. You call an employer or business of your choice, introduce yourself, and ask if you can set up a day where you can come in and job shadow.

Most employees want to share information about their jobs and help students and others learn about career opportunities. If for some reason they say no, call someone else.

Here are a few things a person can learn from a job shadowing experience:

- what really goes on at the workplace
- details of a specific career
- if he or she can do this job
- if he or she wants to do this job
- if there are entry-level positions or if he or she needs experience
- how to interact with others in a career-interest field
- an understanding of the expected qualifications of a prospective employee
- can also obtain a new contact
- if he or she needs to go to college, etc.

Employer Phone Interview

(Another way to find out about jobs and careers)

(Copy and use as your guide)

Date: _____

Company Name: _____

Manager's Name: _____

Phone: _____

Ask for the manager, personnel manager, or the person who does the hiring. When he or she comes to the phone, say, "Hi, my name is_____. I am doing a research paper on your company's hiring process and would like to ask you a few questions, if this is a good time for you. If not, I can call you back."

Sample Questions (great classroom activity too):

What do you look for when you hire someone?

What is an entry-level position?

What are the duties or responsibilities of the job?

What experience is required, if any?

How old do you have to be to work here?

How often do you hire?

How do you advertise your job openings?

How do applicants dress when they apply at your business?

What do the majority of applications look like?

Are you willing to be a guest speaker at my school?

Are you willing to be a training site for some of our school programs, such as internships?

** Make sure you thank the employer for his or her time!

Additional Comments

Networking

According to the HBS Alumni Association, 65 to 85 percent of jobs are secured through networking!

One of the best ways for seeking employment is networking. You want to tell everyone you know that you are looking for a job, including your neighbors, who may be a business owner. Before my son was sixteen, he discovered one of our neighbors had a mail business, and he ended up working for them on weekends when needed.

Many people think the best place to look for a job was in the classified section of the newspaper. It may have been a good source years ago, especially in the Sunday edition, but not anymore. Very few jobs are advertised in the paper now. As most people know, many employment agencies assist people in obtaining employment. However, you need to be careful of those that charge a fee. There are many websites for locating employment. Conducting informational interviews with companies is one of the best tools for finding out what you want and don't want to do, as I have explained. In addition, it can land you a job!

Job shadowing is an old method and remains very effective. When I was still in school, I job shadowed a florist and a veterinary clinic. When I first decided to become a job developer, I followed someone around for a week to find out how she performed the job. I discovered that that was definitely a job I was interested in and wanted to pursue. As soon as a position became available, I applied, was interviewed, and hired! The employer was impressed that I took the time to follow someone around. Being a job developer requires a great deal of organizational skills, time management, and other unique talents. I have had people follow me around, and they are now doing the same job. It is all a matter of what we want to do and how far we are willing to go to obtain what we want. Look around. You will see people who are successful. Talk to them; find out how they did it or pray and let God lead and guide you. There are different paths to success. We all have to follow our own way. Input from others and research is often necessary.

You may research Jack Canfield to find out how he began his career and became a best-selling author, speaker, and trainer. I have met him, read some of his books, and attended some of his online trainings. He said that if he could do it then anyone could.

ROP, which stands for Regional Occupational Program, is another excellent way to find out what you want or don't want to do. Many of the classes include on-the-job training for almost every type of career. Check with your local high schools. Classes are FREE, and the only requirement is that you are at least sixteen years of age. However, some classes will have a fee for books and maybe uniforms. Some classes cater to students first. I taught the ROP customer service class for thirteen years, placing student and adults into jobs for work-experience training. The ones who did well were hired!

There are other ways to network. You may want to try something new or even start your own business. Talk to people who are doing what you want to pursue. You can attend chamber of commerce and Rotary Club meetings and conferences and volunteer on committees. Get involved in alumni associations or join a professional trade association in your field. You can take business connections to lunch. You can write to authors of books and articles in your field or start a new hobby. LinkedIn is a great social network for business contacts. Make sure you have a professional profile. You can make it similar to a résumé. The list is endless.

As the saying goes, "It is not always what you know, but who you know."

100 Ways to Motivate Yourself

Shine

1. Create a vision
2. Tell a true lie
3. Leave your comfort zone
4. Find out your key
5. Plan your work
6. Move your goal post
7. Dribble with another hand
8. Play your character
9. Sit quietly
10. Use the right chemicals
11. Leave high school
12. Loose face
13. Sing without feeling
14. Kill your television
15. Read yourself a story
16. Get on your death bed
17. Be lazy to begin with
18. Leave your friends
19. Plan your game
20. Find your Einstein
21. Feel good first
22. Run toward your fear
23. Be unexpected
24. Create your relationships
25. Be where you are
26. Act like a hero
27. Accept your willpower
28. Say no to yourself

Live

29. Make new word connections
30. De-program yourself
31. Open the present
32. Serve and grow rich
33. Imitate Columbo

34. **Give away some power**
35. **Talk to yourself**
36. **Schedule your comebacks**
37. **Live your true life**
38. **Get up on the right side of the bed**
39. **Use your magic machine**
40. **Get your stars out**
41. **Be a finisher**
42. **Invent Games**
43. **Inner act**
44. **Live a whole life today**
45. **Welcome your problems**
46. **Drive a Library**
47. **Rewind your thoughts**
48. **Create your goals**
49. **Get small**
50. **Get out of the box**

51. **Advertise yourself**
52. **Don't stop thinking**
53. **Debate your dark side**
54. **Make use of trouble**
55. **Learn to Brainstorm by yourself**
56. **Create your own voice**
57. **Live on the frontier**
58. **Replace your habits**
59. **Paint your day**
60. **Swim laps under water**
61. **Coach, watch, evaluate**
62. **Leave home**
63. **Perform rituals**
64. **Start life over**
65. **Keep promises**
66. **Give some luck away**
67. **Draw your universe**
68. **Get up the game**
69. **Turn your mother down**
70. **Face the sun**
71. **Look inside**
72. **Go to war**
73. **Make small change**
74. **Do things badly**
75. **Be a visionaire**

76. **Shine your light**
77. **Be a list writer**
78. **Be the change**
79. **See the goal**
80. **Simplify**
81. **Pin life down**
82. **Strengthen your purpose**
83. **Go on a news fast**
84. **Choose an action**
85. **Be a thinker**
86. **Choose an enjoyment**
87. **Read mystery novels**
88. **Express your thoughts**
89. **Use your weaknesses**
90. **Try becoming your problem**
91. **Inflate your goal**
92. **Come to your rescue**
93. **Push your own buttons**
94. **Strengthen your rehearsal**
95. **Improve your vision**
96. **Build your power base**
97. **Link truth to beauty**
98. **Take no for a question**
99. **Walk with love and death**
100. **Buy yourself flowers**

Motivate

—Steve Chandler

It has been said,

Success is doing what the unsuccessful are unwilling to do.

It is also a journey, not a destination!

"Success is to be measured not so much by the position that one has reached in life as by the obstacles which he has overcome by tying to succeed."

—Booker T. Washington

Chapter 2

Interviews

Three Things That Make A Good Impression During An Interview:

1. How You Look

2. How You Sound

3. What You Have To Say

"Persistence and moral courage don't guarantee victory, but they prevent defeat. In the game of life, we win something every time we overcome our fears."

—Michael Josephson

The Job Interview and First Impressions

(Notes from an Employer)

Employers almost always interview prospective employees in person. The employer wants to meet to find out your ability to communicate, what your personality is like, and what your skills and qualifications are for the job. It is very important that you make a good first impression when you meet the interviewer. Following are some tips to create a good first impression:

1. Be on time or early for the interview. If you are late, the employer may assume that you will always be late for work.
2. Go alone to the interview. Leave friends outside or at home. The boss might think your friends will be visiting you at work or that you lack self-confidence.
3. Before the interview, learn something about the company. Know what products or services are involved. The interviewer may ask what you know about the company.
4. Dress well. Wear clean, ironed clothes. Men can were a tie and a jacket if appropriate. Otherwise, a clean shirt and dress pants are fine. Women can wear dresses, skirts, or pants and add a jacket.
5. Avoid excessive or way-out makeup, clothes, or accessories. This tends to draw attention to the way you look. Stress qualifications, not looks.
6. Never wear sunglasses, especially mirrored sunglasses, to an interview. It gives the impression that you are hiding something and that your answers might not be truthful.
7. Be aware of colors, both good and bad. And it is just as distracting for the interviewer if you wear excessive perfume or aftershave as it is if you forgot to brush your teeth or use deodorant.
8. Express your interest by your walk, so don't lazily stroll into the office. Walking very slowly might give the wrong impression.
9. Stand up straight, hands out of your pockets, and don't lean on the walls or desks. This may give the impression that you are lazy.
10. Sit alert. Don't slouch, as that will make you appear lazy as well.
11. Never sit down until the interviewer offers you a chair. Don't walk in and make yourself at home. This is a formal affair.
12. Shake hands if the interviewer offers. Always shake hands firmly.
13. Speak clearly and loudly enough to be easily heard. A soft, quiet voice gives the impression that you are either shy or slow.
14. Do not chew gum or smoke. Gum chewing distracts from the interview and may annoy the interviewer. Never smoke, even if the opportunity is offered. When

hired, you can work out a place and time to smoke at work. People can be sensitive, so be careful.

15. Avoid acting nervous. Try not to fidget or play with jewelry, your hair, or items on the desk. Relax, stay calm, and be yourself.

16. Watch for reactions from the interviewer. Look for signs of boredom and disbelief. Watch for positive reactions, such as acceptance.

17. Smile and look the interviewer in the eye. Make eye contact when answering questions. This shows sincerity and trust.

18. Use proper English. Avoid slang and arguing. Be frank, truthful, and polite.

19. Don't discuss personal problems.

20. Thank him or her for the interview, shake hands, and leave. It is proper to ask when you will hear if you are hired.

Here are some hints for achieving a good job interview and making a good first impression:

- Be prepared to answer questions before the interview. Think about how you would answer commonly asked questions.
- Be flexible about conditions and hours you will work.
- Be prepared to take a test or to demonstrate a skill.
- Bring samples of your work, letters of recommendation, a résumé, references, or other items to show your skills and qualifications. A portfolio containing these documents would show these materials well. Be prepared to leave the portfolio with the employer if necessary.

Preparing for the Interview

First of all, make sure you wear professional attire. Ladies should always wear a dress or skirt with nylons and closed-toed shoes. Pantsuits are acceptable also. I strongly believe all ladies should own a black jacket, as it will complement any wardrobe. Also it helps to have a black skirt and black dress pants so you can mix and match. Gentlemen should always wear a tie. Ladies and gentlemen, always keep jewelry to a minimum and take out piercings. If you have tattoos, cover them up. Do not smoke before your interview, and do not use too much cologne or perfume. And ladies, please cover your chests!

Bring your résumé and portfolio or anything else you want to share. You should have researched the company prior to the interview. If you want to work for a certain business, go in and look around. See what they sell or what they do. I once had a student who wanted to work at Burlington Coat Factory. She had no idea that they sold more merchandise than coats. (Of course now the name has been changed to Burlington.) An employer could ask you what kind of jeans or handbags his or her company sells; therefore, it is vital you do your homework and find out. That alone could be why you get hired or not!

Always arrive early to the interview!

Prior to the interview, have someone ask you some questions to see how you respond and have him or her give you feedback. (Sample questions are included in this guide.) Another way is to sit in front of a mirror and practice talking about yourself. The number one question in an interview usually is "Can you tell me about yourself?" This should be the easiest question; however, many struggle with it. This is not a test. It is all about *you*! There is no reason not to be able to answer a question about yourself. No one knows you better than you. We all know what we can and cannot do. You should be aware of your skills, strengths, weaknesses, and goals and why you want to work there or how you may fit into that company. If you don't know, ask your family, friends, or teachers. Often they can tell you a great deal about yourself and your qualities.

Memorize some of your attributes, such as

- being organized and focused, taking initiative, being creative and productive with great time-management skills. I have observed throughout my years working with high school students that many do not know what *initiative* means. I then ask them if their parents tell them to clean their room, do the laundry, or empty the trash or can they see those things need to be done and just do it on their own? If they answer the latter, I tell them they can tell an employer that they have initiative. When something needs to be done, they do it without being told.

- giving an example of how you have used teamwork, if you consider yourself a team player. Consider the times you were on a sports team, in a club or group, etc., and explain to the employer how you used teamwork. Make sure to elaborate on your answers and give specific examples to illustrate your point. If you do not understand a question, ask the employer to rephrase it.

Like trying out for the football team, cheerleading, or a play, an interview is a rehearsal. Therefore, you need to practice and prepare. Whether you have a one-on-one interview or a panel, make sure to greet everyone by shaking their hands and smiling. During the interview, you will be asked many questions about your work experience, skills, education, activities, and interests. You will then be assessed as to how you will perform the job in relation to the company objectives.

During the interview, try to relax, sit up straight, and maintain good eye contact. Make sure to show enthusiasm and speak loudly and clearly. Do not cross your arms and do not say "you guys." Address the interviewer by name, sir, or ma'am. Also avoid using "um" too many times. When you have answered the question, stop. Then the employer will know to continue. You don't want to ramble on and on. And don't say, "That's about it."

Closing the Interview

The interview is a two-way process. Often the employer will ask if you have any questions. Never ever say no! Always ask a question that shows interest in the job. You can ask when they may be making a decision, or what their expectations are for the person they want to hire. Do they provide training? Are there opportunities for advancement? You may also highlight any strengths or skills you forgot to mention. Make sure to shake hands again and thank them for their time. When you arrive at home, place a thank-you card or letter in the mail, or e-mail them if it is appropriate. Remember, not everyone goes the extra mile. The thank-you card also allows you to mention what you may have forgotten and that you look forward to the possibility of working for them.

"All the world is a stage, and all men and women are merely players."

—William Shakespeare

PERSONAL STRENGTHS

able to meet deadlines	good with numbers
able to prioritize	honest
able to work under pressure	leader, loyal
able to work well unsupervised	meticulous
assertive	multilingual
bilingual	mechanically inclined
can work independently	multitasker
committed	motivational
considerate	neat, organized
creative, confident	patient, persistent
dedicated	public speaker
delegator	planner, positive
dependable	productive, resourceful
detail oriented	punctual, problem solver
diligent	responsible
disciplined	self-motivated

eager to learn	sense of humor
enthusiastic	strong managerial skills
facilitator	take initiative
fast learner	take on challenges
flexible	team player
follow safety rules	time-management skills
friendly, focused	good verbal and written skills
forward thinker	willing to do extra work to gain valuable experience
goal oriented	willing to follow directions
good communication skills	
good listening skills	

You can use the above attributes to sell yourself in an interview. Memorize at least three of your best qualities and elaborate. You want to give the employer a snapshot of you and your skills. You can also add a few to your résumé.

Some Common Interview Questions

The employer wants to find out

- personal information about you,
- what you can offer the company, and
- what you know about the job.

Following are some questions he or she may ask you during your interview:

1. Can you tell me a little about yourself?
2. What are your strengths?
3. What are your weaknesses?
4. What did you like best and least about previous jobs you have held?
5. What duties did you perform on your last job?
6. Tell me what you think good customer service is.
7. Tell me about a time when you had to deal with an angry person and how you handled the situation.
8. Why should we hire you for this job?
9. Why are you interested in working for our company?
10. Have you ever been a member of a team when someone wasn't doing his or her part? What did you do or say?
11. Do you prefer working alone or as a member of a team?
12. Tell me about a time when you had a lot of work to do within a short time and how you completed it in a timely manner.
13. Tell me about a time when a coworker criticized your work. How did you react?
14. Tell me about the last time you had a problem or received a complaint on your job. How did you handle it?
15. What salary are you looking for?
16. What does teamwork mean to you?
17. Where do you see yourself in five years?
18. What qualities do you look for in a supervisor?
19. What is it about sales that appeals to you?
20. What motivates you to do your best?
21. What books have you read, and who is your favorite author?
22. Tell me how you would start a conversation with a customer to find out his or her needs?

23. Describe a time when you might have suggested a new product or an item to a customer?

24. How do you stay productive at work during a slow time?

25. Describe how you might handle a disagreement with a coworker or a manager.

26. Describe how you handle interruptions when you are busy.

27. Describe a time when you had to deal with two important things at once. What did you do?

28. Tell me about a time when you had to deal with a less-skilled person than yourself. How did you handle it?

29. How do you develop and manage your peer relationships?

30. Can you get recommendations? What will your references say about you?

31. Do you have any questions for me?

Questions You May Want to Ask

A good interview is a two-way process. It is as much an opportunity for you to learn about the potential job and organization as it is for a prospective employer to learn about you. Therefore, you should, feel free to ask questions as well. Always ask questions that show interest and enthusiasm for the job.

Following are some questions you may want to consider:

- Can you describe a typical day in this job?
- What are the expectations for this position?
- How will my performance be evaluated for this job?
- What type of person would be best suited for this position?
- Are there special requirements for this job, e.g., travel, overtime?
- How do you see my skills and experience fitting with the job?
- What are the next steps in this interview process?
- Do you have a probation period?
- Are there opportunities for advancement?
- What is the dress code?
- When do you anticipate making your decision?
- What is more important to you, productivity or creativity?
- How do you evaluate success?
- What kind of orientation program do you have for new employees?
- What are your goals for the company in the next year?
- What skills do I need most to help the team?
- Why is this position vacant?
- Do you have any reservations in hiring me?
- If I were hired, what would you like me to achieve in the first three to six months?

Practice Interview Questions

Write out your answers so you can ponder your responses.

1. Would you tell me something about yourself?

    _____

    _____

    _____

2. Why do you want to work here?

    _____

    _____

    _____

3. What are your strengths? What are your weaknesses?

    _____

    _____

    _____

4. Where do you see yourself in three to five years?

    _____

    _____

    _____

5. How do you spend your spare time?

    _____

    _____

    _____

6. How are you qualified for this job?

    _____

    _____

    _____

7.   What did you like/dislike about your last job?

_____

_____

_____

8.   Give an example of an accomplishment (in your last job or your life).

_____

_____

_____

9.   What word best describes you?

_____

_____

_____

10.   Describe a time you had to work under pressure.

_____

_____

_____

11.   What reward, other than money, motivates you to work hard?

_____

_____

_____

12.   Why did you choose the career for which you are preparing?

_____

_____

_____

13.   How would a former employer or teacher describe you?

_____

_____

_____

14. Describe a major problem you had and how you dealt with it.

_____

_____

_____

15. What talents do you possess that qualify you for this position?

_____

_____

_____

16. Why should I hire you?

_____

_____

_____

17. What can you do for this organization?

_____

_____

_____

18. Do you have any questions regarding this position or our organization?

_____

_____

_____

Mock Interview Rating Questions

Have someone ask you these questions and rate how you did.

		Needs Practice	Fair	Good	Excellent
1.	Tell me about yourself.	1	2	3	4
2.	Why do you want to work for us?	1	2	3	4
3.	What do you believe to be your greatest strength?	1	2	3	4
4.	Do you have any weaknesses? If so, what is your greatest?	1	2	3	4
5.	What would one of your teachers or bosses say about you?	1	2	3	4
6.	What would a friend say about you?	1	2	3	4
7.	What is the most difficult adjustment you have ever had to make?	1	2	3	4
8.	What does good customer service mean to you?	1	2	3	4
9.	Can you give an example of good customer service you have received?	1	2	3	4
10.	How do you handle an angry customer?	1	2	3	4
11.	Define teamwork.	1	2	3	4
12.	If you could change one thing about yourself, what would it be?	1	2	3	4
13.	What accomplishments in your life are you most proud of?	1	2	3	4
14.	What is your personal definition of success?	1	2	3	4
15.	What are your goals/plans for the future?	1	2	3	4
16.	Do you have any questions for us?	1	2	3	4
17.	Made good eye contact	1	2	3	4
18.	Appeared self-confident	1	2	3	4
19.	Firm handshake	1	2	3	4
20.	Gave examples in answers	1	2	3	4
21.	Asked questions	1	2	3	4

Dressed for Interview	Yes ■	No ■
Brought Résumé	Yes ■	No ■
Good Application	Yes ■	No ■

Comments:

_____

_____

_____

_____

_____

Preparing for the Actual Interview
(Questions with possible responses)

Before the Interview

Remember to research the company; find out as much as you can. Also practice and prepare for the interview. Make sure you have professional attire. Ladies, make sure to cover your chests. Interviewers want to make eye contact with you, not the Grand Canyon. Gentlemen should always wear a tie. Everyone should remove piercings and cover all visible tattoos.

Every day, look in the mirror and recite your skills and personal attributes, such as, "I am a very organized, creative person who always takes initiative and has a great work ethic." Give examples of your skills and where you learned them. If you consider yourself a team player, give an example of how you have used teamwork in the past. Elaborate on your responses. Interviews are about selling yourself. Try to put yourself in the employer's shoes. If you had a business, what kind of person would you want to hire? Obviously someone who is loyal and can be depended on.

Make sure to have a résumé, and bring a portfolio of your accomplishments. Or bring samples of past work and projects to share. See what to include in chapter 3.

As always, dress to impress. You do not have a second chance to make a good first impression!

During the Interview

Shake hands with everyone who is at the table in the interview room with you. You will be asked many questions about your work experience, skills, education, activities, and interests. You will be assessed as to how you will perform the job in relation to the company objectives. All your responses should be concise. Use examples to illustrate your point whenever possible. Your responses need to be adapted to the present interview. If you do not understand a question, always ask to have the question rephrased.

Frequently Asked Questions and Responses

"Can you tell me a little about yourself?"

Describe your skills/experience, interests, and background, including what you have learned in past jobs. You can mention any training and education you have received. If you are unsure what information the interviewer is seeking, say, "Are there any areas in particular you'd like to know about?" Don't forget to mention some of your attributes, such as

- I am able to prioritize and meet deadlines.
- I am assertive, dedicated, a fast learner, and goal oriented.
- I consider myself productive, organized, and self-motivated.
- I always take initiative and am always willing to do extra work.
- I am meticulous, mechanically inclined, and resourceful.
- I have great communication skills and work well with others.
- I am disciplined, a team player, and bilingual.

"Do you have any weaknesses? If so, what do you consider one of them?" (Keep in mind, we *all* have weaknesses.)

Select something you are comfortable sharing. You need to turn a weakness into a strength. For example, if you struggle with reading, you can say that you have a tutor to assist you and you read every day. Or that you are a bit shy until you get to know people. Or if you are usually late that you have decided to set your clock thirty minutes ahead so you are early everywhere you go. Or you can say some of the following:

- "I'm something of a perfectionist."
- "I'm a stickler for punctuality."
- "I'm tenacious.
- "I am often too detail oriented."
- "I'm a workaholic."

"What is your greatest strength? What do you feel you are really good at?"

You may respond with any of the following:

- "I work well under pressure and am able to meet deadlines."
- "I am very organized and have great time-management skills."
- "I like being productive and resourceful."
- "I enjoy being creative and coming up with new ideas."
- "I am self-motivated."
- "I am a good multitasker."
- "I consider myself to be a great delegator."
- "I am a problem solver.
- "I always take initiative."
- "I'm a great listener."
- "I am very patient."
- "I consider myself a leader."

"Where do you see yourself in five years? What are your goals?" (The interviewer also wants to know if you plan on sticking around.)

If you are a student, you should have some idea about what you want to do after graduation. If not, you can say, "This is my first job I am applying for and want to get some experience and training, which will hopefully bring me closer to deciding what I may want to do. I hope to still be working here and to have increased my performance level and abilities." Or maybe you just want to obtain some experience in this field to determine your future education and degree. You may be starting out as a paralegal secretary and decide later that you want to become an attorney.

"Why have you been out of work for so long?"

Following are some appropriate responses:

- "I spent some time reevaluating my past experience and the current job market to see what direction I wanted to take."
- "I have been looking for work."
- "I have had job offers, but I am not just looking for another job; I am looking for a career."
- "I took some time off to raise my children."
- "I was a domestic engineer."
- "I went to school."

"What do you know about our company? Why do you want to work here?"

This is where you should have conducted your informational interview beforehand to find out about the company. You need to know what your interests are and why you are choosing this job, which you may convey by the following:

"Your company has superior products and customer service."
"Your company is a leader in the field and is growing."
"You are a small (or large) firm and a leading force in the local/national economy."
"I shop (and/or eat) here."
"I have experience in this field."
I enjoy working with these products/merchandise."
"I travel/visit here frequently."
"I want to learn more about your company or gain more experience in this field."
"I someday hope to open my own business."

"So why should I hire you?" Explain why you are the best person for the job!

Highlight your background based on the company's current needs. Recap some of your qualifications, keeping the interviewer's job description in mind. If you do not have a lot of experience, talk about how your education and training/ROP has prepared you for this job.

"What is your greatest accomplishment?"

Give a specific illustration/example from a previous or current job where you might have saved the company money, helped increase its profits, or anything else. If you are in school or have recently graduated from college, find some accomplishment from your schoolwork, part-time jobs, or extracurricular activities, including sports or personal events, such as, passing a major test, getting a drivers license, graduating, getting a degree, passing an ROP class, perfect attendance, high GPA, awards, purchasing a home, assisting someone in a major crisis, publishing a book, writing a song, making a video, job promotion, and the list goes on.

"Tell me about a problem you had in your last job and how you resolved it."

The employer wants to assess your analytical skills and see if you are a team player. Select a problem or challenge from your past or current job, and explain how you resolved it. If you have never worked before, find another example, such as in school, home, or sport activity, etc.

"Describe a time when you received poor customer service. How did that make you feel? Can you give me an example of good customer service you have received? How would you respond to an angry customer? What does good customer service mean to you?"

We should all treat customers the way we would want to be treated. We may choose to use the Ritz Carlton as an example. Cesar Ritz once said, "The customer is always right and people like to be served, but invisibly." If a guest did not like an entrée, it was whisked from the table. Customers like to be acknowledged and receive courteous and respectful service. It is important to listen to the customer, be sympathetic, and ask questions. Obviously, if you have an angry customer and cannot help him or her, you should direct him or her to your manager.

"Do you have any questions you would like to ask of us?"

Never say no! Again, always ask a question that shows interest and enthusiasm for the job. It is best not to ask about salary, benefits, or vacations. Wait until you have received a job offer. If you did the informational interview beforehand, you will know the answers. But following are some questions you might ask:

- "What is the dress code?"
- "Can you describe what a typical day on the job might be?"
- "Are there opportunities for advancement?"
- "Does your company offer training?"
- "What are your expectations for this position?"
- "What type of person are you looking to hire for this position?"
- "Are there special requirements for this job, such as travel or overtime?"
- "When can I start?" or "When do you anticipate making your decision?"

There is another complete list of examples in this book.

"If we were able to offer you a position, when are you available to start?"

This answer will depend on if you are working currently or not. If you are working now, you want to make sure you give your present employer at least one-to two-week's notice. Therefore, you will need to explain that to the interviewer. You can say, "I am currently working and would like to give my present employer enough notice. How soon would you want me to start?" If you are not working or are going to school, "today" or "tomorrow" would be a great answer. But this truly depends on your commitments. Sometimes the employer is asking this only to see if you will give your present employer notice. That will let him or her know your work ethic. If he or she hires you, he or she will want the same respect.

Closing the Interview

Remember, the interview is a two-way process. This is now your opportunity to inquire about the job. You can ask questions that may not have yet been answered. Highlight any strength you may have forgotten to mention during the interview. Ask when they expect to make their decision. If there is another interview, obtain the necessary information. Thank the interviewer, and shake his or her hand.

Illegal Questions

During an interview, you may be asked some questions that are considered illegal, such as those related to sex, age, race, religion, national origin, marital status, disability, or any inquiries about your personal life that is not relevant to the job.

Sometimes the interviewer may not know the question is illegal. There are, however, age requirements for certain jobs, such as for serving alcohol and operating certain types of machinery.

You need to decide how uncomfortable the question makes you and then determine how you wish to respond. It is perfectly acceptable to respond by saying, "May I ask why you are asking me this question?" or "How is this relevant to the job?" Sometimes an employer may ask if you have children. They are trying to determine how often you might call in due to your kids being ill. In this case, it is usually best to let them know you have dependable child care.

It is okay to say that you do not see the relationship between the question and your qualifications; therefore, you prefer not to answer the question.

Sometimes there will be a second interview.
Some companies conduct group interviews.

After the Interview

Always try to send a thank-you letter or card, thanking them for their time to interview you. In addition, you may mention something else you may have forgotten to tell them. Let them know you look forward to hearing from them or the possibility to work for them.

Once a job offer has been made, you can assess if you really want the job. Does the job meet your requirements? Do they have insurance benefits? If you did not get the job, it is okay to call back and find out why. This will help you with future interviews.

"More of our basic human needs will be simultaneously satisfied through work than any other arena of our lives."

—Sigmund Freud

Why People May Not Get Hired

Sometimes people are not hired because of what they said or did not say. Sometimes it is because their facial expressions or voice quality. Maybe they did not appear confident, rambled too much, or did not show enthusiasm. Body language speaks louder than words. Sometimes employers have already decided who they will hire before the interview but still have to go through the process.

Positive reasons are as follows:

- too many applicants
- an employee changed his or her mind and decided not to leave
- your skills are more than what is needed for the position
- they cannot pay what you are making now
- they are looking for more experience
- they are only accepting applications for a future need
- lack of experience on the part of interviewer
- they are only trying to fill a temporary position

Negative reasons are as follows:

- poor personal appearance
- overbearing, overaggressive, know-it-all attitude
- inability to express yourself clearly; poor voice, poor grammar
- uncommunicative; only gave yes or no responses
- lack of planning for career; no purpose or goals
- lack of interest and enthusiasm; passive, indifferent
- lack of confidence and poise; nervousness, ill at ease
- overemphasis on salary; interest only in dollar offer
- poor grades; just did well enough to pass
- unwilling to start at entry level; expect too much too soon
- made excuses for past work record
- failed to make eye contact with the interviewer
- limp, fishy handshake
- sloppy application
- poor résumé
- want only a temporary position
- late to interview without a valid excuse
- knew nothing about the company
- failure to express appreciation for interviewer's time
- gave indefinite responses to questions

I always recommend calling the employer to find out why you did not get the job so you know how to prepare for the next interview.

> "Success is not final, failure is not fatal; it is the courage to continue that counts."
>
> —Thomas Edison

If You're Offered the Job

Before you accept, evaluate the position carefully in terms of the following:

- ❑ **job responsibilities**
- ❑ **working hours**
- ❑ **pace of work**
- ❑ **advancement opportunities**
- ❑ **salary range**
- ❑ **benefits**

- ❑ **job location**
- ❑ **transportation requirements: Is public transportation available or do you need a car?**
- ❑ **working conditions**
- ❑ **future possibilities: What could the job lead to?**

Even if you have accepted verbally, you may want to write a note thanking the employer or make a follow-up call to confirm your starting date and time. Also know the dress code. Do not assume anything.

Some Bs on How to Keep Your Job

Be Punctual

Always be on time or early; call the employer if you will not be there or if you may be late. Be responsible and show good work ethic, especially if you want to be promoted.

Be Enthusiastic

Always act like you enjoy your job. When you do, you become a more productive worker. Make sure to smile and focus on the positive.

Be an Initiator

Always be ready to find things to do or ask what else you can do. Look busy and always go the extra mile.

Be Conscientious

Be diligent and focused. Avoid gossip. Dress appropriately and show appreciation for others. Do not come to work under the influence. Always use good judgment.

Be Aware of Safety Rules

Employers do not want to keep people who have accidents or who do not follow the safety rules. It is costly and dangerous to others and themselves.

Be a Team player

Assist others, for people depend on one another in work situations. Be able to work in a group. Be goal oriented and have creative ideas, integrity, and leadership skills. Good communication is also essential. There is no "I" in *team*!

Be Respectful

If you do not like your job, look for something else on your days off. Make sure to always give two-week's notice and a letter of resignation. In addition, ask for a letter of reference. Leave things in an organized manner for someone else.

Be Inquisitive

Take courses. Improve your methods. Ask for additional duties or training. Ask for feedback on your performance. Make every effort to grow with your organization.

"People Acting Together as a Group Can Accomplish Things. Which No Individual Acting Alone Could Ever Hope to Bring About."

—Franklin Delano Roosevelt

"Unless you try to do something beyond what you have already mastered, you will never grow."

—Ralph Waldo Emerson

Sample Thank-You Letter

(Or you can write in a card)

[Date]

11407 HireMeLane
Sun Valley, CA 90707

Ms. Robin Rask, Manager
Diamond's Restaurant
7777 Diamond Drive
Sun Valley, CA 90707

Dear Ms. Rask,

I enjoyed the opportunity of meeting with you on June 2 for the cashier / hostess position. The high level of energy among your employees, as well as their personal pride in the restaurant, was obvious.

After touring the restaurant, I realized I have valuable organizational skills that your company will be looking for in an employee. In addition, I am bilingual.

I look forward to the possibility of working for you. Thank you.

Sincerely,

MaryAnn Needy

MaryAnn Needy

Sample Letter of Resignation

[Date]

Mr. Louis Blanker, Manager
McMurray's Restaurant
13245 Poway Road
Poway, CA 92064

Dear Mr. Blanker,

Please accept my resignation from my job as a cashier. My last day of work will be April 15, 2017. I will be accepting a position with more work hours.

I appreciate the wonderful experience and training from McMurray's Restaurant. I have learned many valuable job skills while working with you. I will be more than happy to train my replacement. Thank you for accepting my resignation.

Sincerely,

Sally Brown

Sally Brown

Follow-Ups after the Application, Résumé, and Interview

One of the reasons many job seekers are not successful in obtaining employment is because they do not follow up after applying for the job. Oftentimes they do not follow up even after the interview.

Many job seekers often complain about employers not responding back to them. Employers are not obligated to call you; their purpose is to find the right person for the job. Applications are usually the first impression the employer has of you. It is also a way to weed you out, if it is not filled out completely and neatly. Online applications also need to be filled out completely, and many include assessment tests. If you don't pass the online tests, you will not be considered. Some are easy while some are very challenging. Sometimes you will be notified that you passed, and sometimes you will not. Therefore, it is vital to follow up. Employers then look at your availability and experience.

You may be the right person for the job, but they may not have received your résumé and cover letter in the mail or by fax or e-mail. Another great reason to follow up is to make sure they did. Some employers do not even receive phone messages. I have to call many businesses several times because their staff did not deliver the message. Following up with your application also lets the employer know that you are eager and interested. Most employers receive hundreds of applications and résumés weekly. Again, this is another reason to always follow up.

Applicants often tell me they cannot find a job and that they have been everywhere. When I ask them where they have been, they usually give me about five places. I tell them that they have not been everywhere and need to keep at it until they are hired. I always ask them, "Did you write down where you went, the date you applied, the manager's name, and what was said when you submitted your application and or résumé?" The response almost always is no. I also ask them if they dressed professionally when they applied. Employers may say, "Sorry, we are not hiring right now, but feel free to check back with us." You need to write that down. They may ask you to check back in the near future or call. Make sure you do so.

When looking for a job, I tell my applicants they often need to go to each place three to four times and ask for the same manager to tell them they are interested in working there. If they do not get hired, they need to go to ten other places and do the same thing. There will always be people who quit their job, get fired or promoted, etc. Often it is about being at the right place at the right time. If you are unemployed and looking for work, that needs to be your full-time job. Sometimes when you complete an online application, it is not possible to follow up. But do so whenever possible.

In my younger years, I lived in the mountains and was looking for work. It was very challenging to find what I was looking for in such a remote area. When I could not find the job I wanted, I realized that I had to go almost everywhere and anywhere because I needed a paycheck. I quickly obtained a job and on my days off searched for other jobs. One year I worked three jobs at the same time for six months. It allowed me to save enough money to take my family to Europe. I have almost always worked more than one job at the same time. Sometimes you may have to take a job you do not want to help pay the bills until you find something else.

If you are in your twenties or older, unemployed and not going to school but are able to work and still living at home, obviously something is wrong. It is all a matter of your goals and priorities. If you want something, pursue it! Ask others for help when you need it. Resources are everywhere. Most things take discipline and effort. If you have a disability and want to work, there are plenty of resources to assist you. Some successful attorneys are in wheelchairs. Often the physically disabled are willing to work harder than those who are not.

When my son David came back to live with me after he turned eighteen, I told him he had to have a job and pay one hundred dollars a month for rent and use of my car. He told me he did not know what he wanted to do. I told him to get off his behind and just get a job. Then he would figure it out along the way what he wanted to do or not do. He did just that and then joined the United States Air Force. I am proud to say, David bought his first home at the age of twenty-five. He now has a great job and is using his skills and talents.

Job seekers who fill out applications online will need to follow up with the manager or the human resource department whenever possible and in person. Let him or her know you filled out the application online and are interested in working there and would like to know the next step. Just because you are filling out an application online at Walmart does not mean you should sit there in your pajamas and slippers. Yes, I have seen this, and so have others. You never know who may be watching. One of my employers told me that he has a mirror in his store by customer service where people apply. If he sees someone walk in wearing a suit, he makes time to speak to him. It has been said, "There is no traffic in the extra mile and always give people more then they expect."

When you interview, you will not always get a response indicating that you were not selected. Always follow up anyway, and send a thank-you card or letter. Once I went on an interview that I knew I was qualified for, but I did not get the job. I called them to inquire why I was not selected. They told me I did not show enough enthusiasm. The person they hired did not work out. Six months later, I applied again, was very enthusiastic in the interview, and was hired on the spot. Had I not asked, I would have never known.

Some businesses will interview ten to twenty people but have already selected someone. There's nothing you can do about that except be grateful for the interview experience. The more interviews you go on, the better you become.

With today's technology, you can have job search applications on your mobile devices and set up mobile alerts on job postings. Most people check all their media and social accounts several times a day. Do the same with your job search.

Closing Comments

Be persistent without being a nuisance. Consider the follow-up process as an integral step in your job search.

Printed by Permission by Dan Johnston, PhD.

SMILING FACTS ☺

Do you want a guaranteed way to improve your mood and your health? Try smiling!

Laughter relieves stress and improves the immune system. Laughing has been described as an internal jog. It massages our inner organs and gives them a workout. Smiling exercises fourteen facial muscles. When we laugh, our blood pressure goes up and then comes down. We also stretch our lungs, relax our chests, and breathe easier. Laughter causes our bodies to release neurochemical compounds associated with an improved mood. When we laugh, we change our perspective and attitude.

Research has found that four-year-old children smile and laugh about four hundred times a day while for some adults smiling and laughter decreases to only fourteen times a day. What happens between childhood and adulthood? Maybe as we become serious, hardworking adults, we lose our sense of humor along with the freedom to laugh. Such a loss is unfortunate because humor can be healing.

Forcing yourself to smile may work almost as well as laughing; at least, it may change your mood. Putting a big smile on your face sends a message to your brain that things are okay. If you are smiling, your brain thinks, *I must be happy!*

Smile on purpose, even if you don't feel like it. See if you can fool yourself into a good mood. As the saying goes, "Fake it until you make it."

BE SURE TO SMILE TODAY!

Chapter 3

Résumé

How to Compose Your Résumé

The following procedure will help:

1. Recheck your list of accomplishments, abilities, skills, qualifications, etc.
2. Decide on your main job objectives.
3. Choose a format:
   - ❑ Chronological lists employment history in reverse order of time (most common style).
   - ❑ Functional emphasizes skills.
   - ❑ Combination covers both functional and chronological information.

> This is your personal inventory and formal introduction to a potential employer.

4. Include:
   - ❑ Name, address, telephone number(s), and e-mail address at the top
   - ❑ Objective, summary, or profile
   - ❑ Employment history
   - ❑ Educational background
   - ❑ Optional (depending on space): volunteer work, language skills, memberships, academic honors, awards, activities, hobbies, etc.
5. Edit to make it easy to read. (Try to keep it to one page.) Include only the most important information. Use perfect spelling, grammar, and punctuation.
6. Type a good final copy. (Make sure to have extra ones printed.) Also place one in your portfolio.

> Résumés come in many styles.
> Ask for assistance. Develop
> the style best for you!

Preparing Your Résumé

If you are looking for a job, you will need a résumé. There are a few opinions on how to write one. The key is to list the experience you have for the job you are applying for. If you have never worked before, your résumé will be more generic, as you will list what you do know and have experience in. Many employers will be looking for key words. Your résumé should speak to today's economic and industry trends and may be written as a story.

Most high school and college graduates have learned practical skills in the classroom and through internships, sports, sororities, volunteer programs, and part-time jobs.

Employers will look for you on social media, websites, or a blog. Therefore, you may want to include links to your personal domain or online portfolio.

Depending on which social media you use, make sure it is professional. Be very careful what you post because it can derail you from obtaining employment. Hiring managers now use social media to screen potential candidates. They look for a professional image and a reason *not* to hire someone.

A résumé is a brief summary of your skills. The general rule is to keep it to one page if possible. However, those who have an array of experience and are seeking a management or higher position will have more information; therefore, their résumés will be two pages.

Your résumé needs to be easy to read and to the point. There are three types: chronological, functional, and a combination of both. Depending on your experience, you will need to decide which format is best for you. I like to use and teach the functional résumé because it works best for those who have a lot of experience, those who have little or no experience, and those who have been out of work for several years.

The chronological format shows the year you started until the year you left, which is not necessary since that information will be on your application. The combination format allows you to list dates and add a skill section for all your other experience and things you can do. The functional résumé gets right to the point and allows you more room to elaborate on your skills. Try to tailor your résumé to the job.

Never use the word "I" on your résumé unless you are adding a summary of qualifications. Always use action words or key phrases that describe what you have done or can do, such as

- goal oriented, self-motivated, and organized
- experienced in Power Point, Word, Excel, Access, Outlook, and Exchange
- create backup and recovery tapes for system applications

- responsible for training and hiring new employees
- knowledge of computer hardware diagnostic troubleshooting
- proficient in LA, WAN, and network installation, monitor, and programming
- used MS Power Point to prepare and deliver presentations to higher echelons
- comp TIA A+ Certification
- active military security clearance
- created and maintain websites
- employee of the month
- volunteer for Red Cross and in charge of fund-raising
- type 80 wpm
- excellent communication skills and bilingual
- in charge of inventory control
- produced 8,428 thirty-second TV commercials
- served as freelance producer and consultant
- multitasker with great time-management skills
- leadership abilities and ability to delegate assignments

No matter what format you choose, the following four things need to be on every résumé. "References upon request" at the bottom is no longer needed. Just make sure you have them typed up on a separate page.

1. Personal information. This is your name, address, phone number(s), and may include an e-mail address (make sure it is professional).

2. Objective. This is the type of job you want to apply for, or make it open enough so you can take your résumé anywhere. Or use a summary of qualifications/profile or both. You may want to consider customizing your summary for each position you apply for.

You do have some creativity with your résumé. However, try to stick with the original black and easy-to-read fonts. Use white or off-white paper. Include relevant information but no redundancies. Do not include pictures unless you are applying for a modeling position and they are requested. Outline your accomplishments, be honest, and use buzzwords sparingly.

You can use a headliner and list an achievement to grab their attention with a sizzle. For example:

Employment Specialist

Trained employees, taught employment skills, and placed applicants into jobs weekly.

3.   Work experience. The employer wants to know where you worked, your job title, and duties performed. Make sure to include volunteer work. Also list any additional skills you have, including being bilingual.

4.   Education. Start from high school and go up: colleges degrees (include ROP classes), GPA awards, certifications, ROTC, teacher assistant, ASB, sports, affiliations, activities, clubs, CPR, cheerleading, food handler's card, fork lift certificate, band, etc. (Brag about yourself.)

Make sure to have a typed list of three to five references in your work portfolio and take to your interview.

When I teach people how to write their résumé, I ask them to start with an outline of the four components above. Then just fill in the blanks. (See the following examples.)

Every time your address, phone number, or e-mail changes, or you gain more experience, you need to update your résumé. After you start your new job, add it to your résumé. Your résumé should always be ready and updated for the next job.

Outline / Functional Format

(Just fill in the blanks)

MaryAnn Needy
1407 Hire Me Lane
Sun Valley, CA 90707
Phone:
MaryannNeedy@yahoo.com

OBJECTIVE: Seeking a position as a Sales Associate

SKILLS / ABILITIES (List your skills and duties you have performed on jobs, if you are bilingual, and three professional traits.)

*

*

*

*

EXPERIENCE (List job title and name of company you worked for. Include volunteer, child care, fund-raising, yard work for neighbors, etc.)

*

*

*

*

EDUCATION (This refers to high school and college. Include TPP, ROP, ROTC, GPA, awards, clubs, sports, organizations, certifications, and if you were a TA.)

EXTRA CURRICULAR ACTIVITIES / SPECIAL INTEREST

Résumé Sample

Completed Outline / Functional Format

MaryAnn Needy
1407 Hire Me Lane
Sun Valley, CA 90707
Phone:
MaryannNeedy@yahoo.com

OBJECTIVE: Seeking an entry-level position where I can utilize my skills and abilities with a company that has opportunity for cross training and advancement.

SKILLS / ABILITIES

- in charge of inventory and customer service
- seated and greeted customers
- operated cash register and collected money for fund-raisers
- assisted with customer carry-outs, bagged groceries, returned merchandise to shelves, swept floors, blocked merchandise, and ran for customer price checks
- delivered newspapers and collected money for customer billing
- assisted teachers with call slips, ran errands, and graded papers
- typing and computer skills, operated copy and fax machines, and set appointments
- in charge of filing documents, data entry, and taking accurate phone messages
- supervised small children, planned meals and activities, and read stories
- CPR certified
- bilingual
- able to work under pressure and complete tasks in a timely manner
- dedicated, focused, forward thinker, and eager to take on new challenges

EXPERIENCE

- sales associate at Sears
- hostess at Marie Callender's Restaurant
- courtesy clerk at Stater Brothers
- office assistant at Desert Valley Dental
- teacher's assistant at Sun Valley High School
- child care provider for neighbors
- volunteer at the Red Cross
- washed and waxed cars for neighbors

- snack bar attendant for the High Desert Soccer League
- newspaper carrier for the *Daily Press*

EDUCATION

Sun Valley High School Diploma

Sun Valley College

EMT and customer service ROP class

cheerleader, annual staff, and TPP career class

GPA 4.0, honor roll, and perfect attendance

ACTIVITIES

Volunteer and assist with the homeless shelters. Enjoy reading and writing. Play guitar and enjoy cooking.

Aim of Resume

The goal is to bring you to the interview stage.

Display your skills, experience. and accomplishments.

Consider

Preparing several resumes, each designed for a special job or company.

Sample Resume

MaryAnn Needy
1407 Hire Me Lane
Sun Valley, CA 90707
Phone:
Email:

Objective: To apply business skills acquired in class and during part-time employment to a full-time office position.

Experience:

2015- Present   Bank Teller / Bank of America
     Duties: Performed basic teller transactions, responsible for balancing cash drawer and providing quality customer service.

2009-2014   Vons Grocery Store / Courtesy Clerk & Cashier
     Duties: Trained new employees and operated cash register. Responsible for carry outs, collected shopping carts and bagged groceries.

Skills

Trained in Word, Excel & Power Point
Typing skills at 80 wpm
Knowledge of office machines
Fluent in Spanish.
Excellent organizational and Time Management skills

Education

Sun Valley High School
Sun Valley College
Teacher Assistant
R.O.P. Financial & Office Occupations
Named outstanding student of the year

Personal Interests

Chess, sailing, reading, writing and assisting others.

Contact Your References

- ❑   **Get their permission before you give their names.**
- ❑   **Select references who are most appropriate for the job you're applying for.**

MaryAnn Needy

1407 Hire Me Lane

Sun Valley, CA 90707

Phone:

MaryannNeedy@yahoo.com

KEYWORDS

Job specialist, job developer, trainer, mentor, time management, organizer, facilitator, monitor, productive, delegator, designer, creative, job coach, PowerPoint, curriculum developer, willing to relocate

PROFILE AND OBJECTIVE

Highly motivated and energetic with excellent organization and time-management skills. Pursuing a position as an employment specialist.

SKILLS AND ABILITIES

- ➢ Excellent in organizing, marketing, delegating, and time-management skills
- ➢ Over 25 years experience in job matching students and adults into employment
- ➢ Designed, coordinated, and facilitated employer seminars and apprenticeship forums
- ➢ Teach employability skills, job club, workshops, and work ethics
- ➢ Developed, facilitated, organized, and implemented annual resource fairs
- ➢ Created employer database
- ➢ Developed and implemented programs and job clubs for students
- ➢ Write and revise student résumés
- ➢ Design and print student certificates
- ➢ Monitor student progress and network with employers
- ➢ Developed curriculum books, resource manuals, and handbooks for employment
- ➢ Created a 15-page-plus ongoing job bulletin/websites to share with job seekers
- ➢ Created Power Point presentations
- ➢ Created and set up vision boards and job boards for classrooms and offices
- ➢ Distribute and share employment information and resources regularly
- ➢ Established and maintain community business partners
- ➢ Organize outstanding students/consumers recognition awards

- Maintain proper documentation, write case notes and reports, and conduct follow-ups
- Responsible for job coaching, career guidance, and assessments
- Conduct job coach orientations and supervise job coaches
- Drafted news releases for newspapers and write newsletters
- Computer literate, multitask-oriented, focused, creative, and productive
- Set up and organize advisory committees and arrange for guest speakers
- Supervised and prepared schedules for nine public relations representatives
- Teach retail and customer service skills and conduct mock interviews
- Assisted in creating Jobsavailableforyou.com website
- Wrote weekly newspaper columns for four months on employment
- Written and published books
- Attend ongoing professional growth conferences
- Landscaping, decorating, and domestic engineering skills
- Coordinate ongoing scholarships
- Member of the H.D. Employment Services Network and the One Stop Career Center
- Served on the board of directors for Job Opportunities and Benefits (JOB)

WORK EXPERIENCE

- Job developer for local high schools
- Employment specialist for the WIA program
- ROP instructor for sales and merchandising
- ROP instructor for diversified occupations and customer service
- Job placement mentor for St. John of God Health Care Services
- Trainer for the independent living skills program
- Recruitment placement specialist for the WorkAbility program
- Recruitment placement specialist for ROP
- Summer youth counselor for JTPA
- Public relations representative for Sun Valley Lodge
- Public relations representative and manager for Lakeview timeshare
- Volunteer committee member for colleges
- Bank teller for Bank of America
- Sales associate and fashion coordinator for clothing outlet
- Retail clerk for Stater Brothers
- Independent contractor/instructor for High Desert College
- Transition advisory board member/scholarship coordinator
- Nerium business consultant

EDUCATION

Vocational education teaching credential, LA County of Education / USD (personnel administration occupations)

BA, liberal arts in fashion merchandising

Professional-growth units and CLAD certified

Business classes at Valley College

Outstanding Student and Teacher of the Year awards

Laguna Hills High School diploma with honors

Resume Key Phrases

Key phrases that will catch the attention of potential employers. Below are some descriptive comments you may include in your résumé, application, or interview to describe your personality, experience, and abilities.

goal oriented

self-motivated and multitask oriented

well organized and enjoy challenges

work well with others

reliable, prompt, determined

able to learn quickly, dedicated

able to meet deadlines

strong managerial and delegating skills

resourceful, problem solver

enthusiastic team member

able to work under pressure

take pride in a job well done

outstanding leadership skills

strong sense of responsibility

good with numbers and figures

committed to completing a job

excellent communication and time-management skills

able to work well unsupervised

able to prioritize a heavy workload

Action Words

(Use in place of "I" to describe what you have done or can do.)

You may find this list helpful when writing a résumé or listing your accomplishments.

➤ Achieved	➤ Delegated	➤ inspected	➤ purchased
➤ acquired	➤ delivered	➤ installed	➤ questioned
➤ adapted	➤ demonstrated	➤ instituted	➤ read
➤ addressed	➤ designed	➤ instructed	➤ realized
➤ administered	➤ detected	➤ insured	➤ received
➤ advised	➤ developed	➤ interpreted	➤ recommended
➤ analyzed	➤ devised	➤ interviewed	➤ recorded
➤ anticipated	➤ diagnosed	➤ invented	➤ recruited
➤ appraised	➤ directed	➤ investigated	➤ reduced
➤ arbitrated	➤ discovered	➤ launched	➤ rehabilitated
➤ arranged	➤ dispensed	➤ lectured	➤ reorganized
➤ assembled	➤ displayed	➤ listened	➤ repaired
➤ assisted	➤ disproved	➤ located	➤ reported
➤ audited	➤ distributed	➤ logged	➤ represented
➤ awarded	➤ doubled	➤ maintained	➤ researched
➤ budgeted	➤ drafted	➤ managed	➤ resolved
➤ built	➤ drew up	➤ mapped	➤ restored
➤ calculated	➤ edited	➤ marketed	➤ reviewed
➤ centralized	➤ eliminated	➤ measured	➤ rewrote
➤ changed	➤ endured	➤ meditated	➤ routed
➤ charted	➤ enforced	➤ minimized	➤ scheduled
➤ classified	➤ established	➤ monitored	➤ selected
➤ coached	➤ estimated	➤ motivated	➤ separated
➤ collaborated	➤ evaluated	➤ navigated	➤ served
➤ collected	➤ examined	➤ negotiated	➤ set up
➤ compiled	➤ exhibited	➤ observed	➤ simplified
➤ completed	➤ expanded	➤ obtained	➤ sketched
➤ composed	➤ explained	➤ operated	➤ sold
➤ compounded	➤ expressed	➤ organized	➤ solved
➤ conceptualized	➤ facilitated	➤ originated	➤ spoke
➤ condensed	➤ forecasted	➤ oversaw	➤ staffed
➤ conducted	➤ formed	➤ performed	➤ studied
➤ confronted	➤ formulated	➤ persuaded	➤ supervised
➤ conserved	➤ found	➤ planned	➤ supplied

- constructed
- consulted
- contracted
- controlled
- converted
- coordinated
- corresponded
- counseled
- created
- criticized
- cultivated
- dealt with
- decided

- founded
- gathered
- generated
- guided
- handled
- handled complaints
- handled detail work
- hired
- identified
- implemented
- improved
- informed
- initiated

- predicted
- prepared
- presented
- prevented
- printed
- processed
- produced
- promoted
- proposed
- protected
- provided
- publicized
- published

- surveyed
- taught
- tested
- timed
- tolerated
- trained
- translated
- treated
- trouble-shot
- updated
- utilized
- worked
- wrote

Resume Writing Skills

Following are some sample job objectives for your résumé:

Objectives

- Motivated student with computer training seeking summer employment in the health care field.

- Seeking a position as a nurse's assistant.

- To pursue a career with a progressive organization in a responsible and challenging position utilizing my experience and skills.

- Seeking an entry-level customer services-related position in a challenging environment that provides opportunity for advancement.

- Seeking part-time or full-time employment.

- Professional career in the area of administration or public relations with an established firm who will utilize my positive attitude, leadership abilities, and communication skills.

- Energetic high school graduate with excellent communication and organizational skills pursuing a career in specialty or technical marketing.

- Energetic college student with excellent communication and organizational skills pursuing a career in accounting or related position in a financial environment.

- Position as an electronics engineering technician. Over eight years of experience in electronics, including design, modification, and technical support of SATCOM, computer hardware/software, communication, radar, and navigation systems. An exceptional technician consistently recognized for money-saving solutions to complex technical problems.

- To obtain a challenging position with a progressive company that can use my experiences and my liberal arts education.

- To obtain a challenging position with a progressive company that has opportunity for cross training and advancement.

- To contribute positively to the public relations effort of a dynamic company.

Summary and or Profile

A summary is a list of a few of your achievements and qualifications that should precede your work history or functional skills. It is a great way to grab attention and inspire the reader. Following are some examples:

- Effective problem solver using excellent verbal and written communications skills.

- Excellent track record for generating overall cost for education and operation efficiency improvements.

- MBA from Harvard University in business management

- Strong leadership skills while advancing team player approach.

- Successfully managed budgets in excess of $3 million.

- Poses special talent for identifying client's needs and presenting effective solutions.

- Fifteen years of proven leadership abilities with an excellent record of achievement.

- Energetic college student with excellent organizational and interpersonal skills pursuing a career in research development.

- Human resources professional with extensive experience in administrative duties seeking a similar position.

- Challenge-driven professional with strong technical skills and history of troubleshooting and problem solving that address complex issues. Consistent record of obtaining goals. Skilled in marketing and public relations.

Scannable Résumé

There are a few different ways you can write your résumé: chronological format, functional format, or a combination of both. You may also choose to have your résumé scanned so you can use the scannable format. You will need to decide which works best for you.

A growing number of companies are using software packages to store, track, and search the résumés they receive. That means computers are now viewing your résumé more than humans, so you can scan your résumé online and reach more companies. Career Builders is very effective.

If you submit your résumé to a company and are not sure if they scan résumés, you can always call the human resource department or personnel office first.

In place of writing out your objective, or in addition to on your résumé, write the word *Keywords* as a heading, either above or below your objective. Under "Keywords" you want to use words that catch the attention of search engines based on the skills, degrees, and experience. You need to find out what the keywords are for the job you are seeking. If there is a job posting or announcement, there may be keywords enclosed on the job description you can use.

When you mail your résumé to a company, if you have keywords listed, they can scan it right into their database. Then if it meets the employer's needs, it will be pulled up for review and you may receive an interview. If you are not sure how to do this, ask someone for assistance. There are many programs and agencies that assist people in finding jobs. Following is an example of how to use the Keyword section on your résumé:

Keywords

human resources, management, organizational skills, administrative assistant, supervisor, program coordinator, time-management skills, leader, team player, honor student, IBM, MS Word, spreadsheet, PowerPoint, desktop publishing, bilingual, PhD, willing to relocate

Résumé Sample

Scannable Format

MaryAnn Needy

1407 Hire Me Lane

Sun Valley, CA 90707

(613) 000-0000

<u>MaryannNeedy@yahoo.com</u>

Keywords

customer service, office assistant, time management, organizational skills, bilingual, team player, computer literate, money management, trained new employees, willing to train, willing to relocate.

Objective

Seeking an office assistant position that will utilize my computer and organizational skills and lead to increased responsibility and advancement.

Education

Cal State San Bernardino, San Bernardino, California—Currently attending for business administration degree

Sun Valley High School, Sun Valley, California

ROP financial and office occupations classes

Computer experience and training: Word, Excel, and PowerPoint

Relevant coursework: general office practices, training and development, transactions and computer applications.

Experience

Bank of America, Sun Valley, California

January 2015–Present

Bank Teller

Performed basic teller transactions, responsible for balancing cash drawers and providing quality customer service.

Achievements and Activities

Outstanding Student of the Year, dean's list, volunteer community assistant, Employee of the Month, tennis coach.

Work Portfolio

This may include the following:

- drawings
- actual product samples small enough to be brought into the interview
- paper samples of work
- photographs that document work with descriptions of planning and progress to completion

Materials to include in your portfolio are

sample of completed job application
résumé
letters of recommendation
certificates/awards
references with addresses and phone numbers
copy of high school diploma
colleges, private schools
transcripts (only if proud)
list of elective subjects with course descriptions
report cards for high school students with 3.0 or better
list of paid work experience
list of unpaid work experience and volunteer work
vocational training/internships and externships
ROP classes
Job Corps, California Conservation Corp, Armed Services
JTPA / WIA / Workability, TPP
adult-supported employment programs
pictures of accomplishments, things you have done, clubs
organizations, outside activities, community service
test results/assessments
examples of how you use teamwork
other

Personal References

Be prepared for your job search by lining up at least three (3) personal references, people who know you well and will speak highly of your character. Do not list relatives as personal references.

List three (3) personal references below. It is very important that you get permission from the individuals listed to use their names as references.

1. _____   _____
    Name   Telephone Number

   _____   _____
    Address   Occupation

   _____   _____
    City / State / Zip   Years Known

. . . .

2. _____   _____
    Name   Telephone Number

   _____   _____
    Address   Occupation

   _____   _____
    City / State / Zip   Years Known

. . . .

3. _____   _____
   Name   Telephone Number

   _____   _____
   Address   Occupation

   _____   _____
   City / State / Zip   Years Known

Letters of Recommendation

Your portfolio should include letters of recommendation. You should ask people who know you and your personality, attitude, and skills. These individuals may be from your list of personal references, current or past employers, teachers, coaches, counselors, or your minister. *Letters of recommendation cannot be from relatives.*

Instructions:

- ❏ Letters must be typed. (If handwritten, type it and have the writer sign it.)
- ❏ The letter should be addressed "To Whom It May Concern."
- ❏ The letter should be written to a prospective future employer recommending you for a job because of your skills, habits, personality, and other attributes known by the writer.

Sample Letter of Recommendation

To Whom It May Concern:

I am writing this letter on behalf of Shauna Davis. Shauna worked for me during the summer of 2016 at my real estate office. She was a great help in reorganizing our files, answering phones, typing, and giving assistance to customers. Shauna has the ability to use computers and knows some common software programs. She is very dedicated, reliable, and productive.

I believe Shauna would be an excellent employee, and I highly recommend her to future employers. She will be an asset to any business that hires her. Please feel free to give me a call at 955-0000 if I may be of assistance or answer any questions about Shauna.

Sincerely,

Robin L. Rask

Robin L. Rask

Sample Cover Letter

Date

Ms. Robin Rask
Executive Vice-President and CEO
Diamond Design Industries
7777 Diamond Drive
Sun Valley, CA 90707

Dear Ms. Rask:

It is with interest and enthusiasm that I am applying for a position as an assistant sales representative. I have acquired excellent retail/merchandising skills in a class I recently completed offered by the county Regional Occupational Program (ROP). I believe the hands-on experience I received will be of particular interest to you.

I have enclosed my résumé and a copy of my ROP certificate for your review.

I have always admired the Diamond Design Industries fashion line and am confident that you can use someone with my particular background, skills, and abilities. I look forward to hearing from you regarding a personal interview.

Thank you for your time and consideration.

Sincerely,

MaryAnn Needy

MaryAnn Needy
1407 Hire Me Lane
Sun Valley, CA 90707
(613) 000-0000

Enclosures: résumé, ROP certificate

A Poem for Computer Users over Forty

A computer was something on TV

From a Science Fiction show of note

A Window was something you hated to clean

And Ram was the father of a goat.

Meg was the name of my girlfriend

And Gig was a job for the nights

Now they all mean different things

And that really Mega Bytes.

An Application was for employment

A Program was a TV Show

A Cursor used profanity

A Keyboard was a piano.

A Memory was something that you lost with age

A CD was a bank account;

And if you had a 3-inch floppy

You hoped nobody found out.

Compress was something you did to the garbage

Not something you did to a file

And if you Unzipped anything in public

You'd be in jail for a while.

Log on was adding wood to the fire

Hard drive was a long trip on the road

A Mouse pad was where a mouse lived

And a Backup happened to your commode.

Cut you did with a pocket-knife

Paste you did with glue

A Web was a spider's home

And a Virus was the flu.

I guess I'll stick to my pad and paper

And the Memory in my head.

I hear nobody's been killed in a Computer crash

But when it happens they wish they were dead.

—Anonymous

Chapter 4

Work Ethics

What Is or Are Work Ethics?

They are a lot of things, but following are some examples.

Your employer pays you to do a job, which means he or she can expect you to

- be on time for work and arrive ready to work;
- call employer if you cannot be at work or will be late;
- be responsible and cooperative;
- be a team player by working well with others;
- follow directions and respond to suggestions;
- represent the business you work for in a positive way;
- be honest/have integrity;
- have good attendance;
- take care of company tools and equipment;
- follow company rules of conduct and all safety rules;
- be neat, dress appropriately, and respect others;
- show initiative, motivation, and enthusiasm;
- stay off cell phones and wear a watch; and
- work safely and have a good attitude.

(Researched / Anonymous)

What is ethics?

Ethics is a standard of conduct that defines behavior based on moral duties and virtue derived from principles of right and wrong.

What is work ethics?

Work ethics is the application of moral standards to practical attitudes and behavior in work situations.

Why learn about work ethics?

Learning about work ethics is important because having good work ethics is an expected behavior in our society. Our very freedom and opportunity for life, liberty and pursuit of happiness depends on good ethics and responsible, right relationships. Good work ethics is the foundation upon which our social-economic system is based, and it supports the pillars of democracy and capitalism in our great society.

Robin Rask

Do young people need to study ethics?

A 1992 study by the Josephson Institute reported that there was a hole in the moral ozone and it was getting larger. A follow-up study in 1996 concluded this hole was indeed getting larger. Unacceptably high numbers of young people consistently act dishonestly and are increasingly prone to violence. Far too many people steal, lie and cheat on the job, in school and in personal relationships. There is a growing and disturbing willingness to resolve conflict with physical force.

The 1996 study of high school showed:

- 65% admitted they had cheated on an exam in the previous year and 47% said they had done so more than once.
- 73 said they lied to their parents more than once.
- 42% of high school males and 31% of high school females said they had stolen something from a store.
- 29% confessed they had stolen something from a parent or relative.
- 55% of high school males and 36% of females said it is sometimes justified to respond to an insult or verbal abuse with physical force.

Learning about good ethics and gaining an appreciation for acceptable behavior can help young people as individuals and as employees on the job. Young people are the foundation of America, and each generation can produce involved, caring citizens with good moral character. Learning about core values: trustworthiness, respect, responsibility, fairness, caring, and citizenship, and practicing these values is important to everyone!

Ten Keys to Listening

(Anonymous & revised)

God made two ears and one mouth, so we could do twice as much listening!! Use the following tips to listen well:

1. Use listening responses, i.e., an occasional "yes," "I see," etc. This shows the employer you are listening and prompts him or her to continue speaking.

2. Take notes. This helps you to remember important points.

3. Prepare in advance. Remarks and questions for employers should be prepared in advance so as to free your mind for listening.

4. Ask questions. If you are not sure that you understood what the employer has said, or feel you have missed an important point, ask him or her to repeat it.

5. Reflect and paraphrase. When you want an employer to further elaborate on a point, use a reflecting phrase, such as, "you said," "you mentioned," or "you described." After repeating the statement as you perceived it, follow through with a question beginning with who, what, where, when, why, or how.

6. Limit your own talking. Remember, you can't talk and listen at the same time.

7. Don't jump to conclusions. Avoid making assumptions about what the employer is going to say or mentally trying to complete sentences for him or her.

8. Don't argue. Do not allow your irritation of things the employer has said, or the manner in which they were said, to distract you from the conversation.

9. Concentrate. Focus on what the employer is saying. Practice shutting out distractions.

10. Don't interrupt. A pause, even a long pause, doesn't mean the employer has finished speaking. Often, conversations and discussions will open up when the person speaking is allowed time to collect his or her thoughts and expand.

Listening to Oral Instructions

Listen carefully. Give your full attention to the person giving you the instructions. Don't be doing something else or thinking about other things. Try to block out background noise or activities.

Listen for the main points. Instructions are not always given in a clear way. If you are not clear as to what you are supposed to do, ask. Find out what is expected of you before you begin.

Listen for the order of the instructions. Often the order in which you do things can make a big difference, so pay attention to words like *first, second, then, next.*

Take notes. Often your supervisor may give you so many instructions at once that it's impossible to remember them all without taking notes. Write down detailed instructions, numbers, and names (ask for spelling of unusual names). John Thompson won't appreciate receiving letters addressed to Tom Johnson.

Think ahead. What problems could arise? What could go wrong? Ask what you should do if certain problems arise.

Repeat the instructions. Be certain that you have understood instructions correctly. This is especially important with numbers.

Deadline. Ask when the task needs to be completed.

Ten+ Most Wanted List

What Employers Are Looking for in Young Adults

A HIGH SCHOOL DIPLOMA	When you tell an employer you stuck to it and got your high school diploma, you are saying you can stick to the job too. To an employer, a G.E.D. may mean you took the easy way out and may not last long on the job.
ABILITY TO PASS A DRUG TEST	Few employers will hire you without asking you to submit to a drug test. If you can't pass a pre-employment drug test, you may not want to apply for a job.
ABILITY TO PASS A CRIMINAL BACKGROUND CHECK	Even a minor shoplifting conviction can prevent you from landing an entry-level job for years to come. If you do have a police record to explain, be honest and tell the employer how the experience has changed you for the better.
A GOOD ATTITUDE	An employer wants people who have a positive attitude and outlook, someone who will contribute to a pleasant work place. Show motivation, enthusiasm, and initiative. Go the extra mile!
BASIC COMPUTER SKILLS	Basic computer skills are easy to get and are required on most jobs today. Having even some computer skills will separate you from the crowd.
BASIC MATH SKILLS	Life is hard without basic math skills. With certain jobs you need to know how to read a ruler, how to add, subtract, multiply, and divide. And don't forget decimals and fractions .
GOOD COMMUNICATION SKILLS	When you talk to an employer, use a more formal approach and remember that the casual language you use with friends; may be offensive to the boss. Make sure to have a professional voice mail message too!
NO VISIBLE TATTOOS OR BODY PIERCING	Since you don't know how your employer feels about tattoos and body piercings, cover them up if you can. Why take the chance of losing a good job over them?
ABILITY TO UNDERSTAND WRITTEN DIRECTIONS	If you have trouble with reading, get help. The ability to read well is the key to having a job that is going somewhere.

ABILITY TO WRITE	You may be the smartest person on the job but if you can't spell or write a sentence, how will the employer know you are smart? Many employers will look at misspelled words on an application as an indication that a person won't be right for the job.
WORK ETHICS AND CUSTOMER SERVICE	Integrity, Loyalty, Honesty, Responsibility, Empathy, Confidentiality, and Respect are just some of the qualities required for success. "The Golden Rule": Treat others, as you would like to be treated. (Anonymous). Has also been modified.

More Employer Expectations

Employers expect the following in their employees:

- adaptability. The ability to make changes smoothly or to successfully adjust to changes that happen in the company. Many of us have stated that every time we get used to something it changes. Remember, change is inevitable, good, and often needed; therefore, we need to embrace it.

- attendance and dependability. Always be punctual. This includes breaks and lunches. Poor attendance costs the employer money. Also dress appropriately for the job, wear a watch, and stay off your cell phone as much as possible.

- basic skills. Employers want people who can read, write, have good math acumen, and can solve problems. These are important skills to have BEFORE you start a job.

- commitment and integrity. The ability to stick to a job or task until it is done. Do what you say you will do and do what is right. If the company has an honor system where you can make your own schedule, make sure you are where you are supposed to be because sometimes they will check on you. Including street sign holders.

- communication skills. The ability to listen to and communicate with others verbally and in writing. Also use good manners and proper language.

- company rules. Know the company policies and procedures regarding absences, tardiness, breaks, dress codes, vacations, sick leaves, telephone use, etc. Find out if the company has a procedure manual.

- customer service. Always treat customers as guests and like you would want to be treated. If a customer is angry, always apologize, and listen to and assist him or her the best you can. If you cannot help, call your supervisor to assist.

- equipment. Learn how to handle machines, tools, and equipment safely to prevent accidents and take care of them properly. This includes equipment you get to keep in your car or take home.

- no gossip. Gossip and rumors can stop with one person: you. Gossip hurts the whole office. Remember, if you cannot say anything good, don't say anything at all.

It has been said,

Five things to THINK about before spreading gossip are:

T: Is it true?

H: Is it helpful?

I: Is it inspired?

N: Is it necessary?

K: Is it kind?

- good judgment. You need to think about a problem and then come to the right decision. Also thinking about which words and actions are right for a situation and which are not. Good judgment is a sign of maturity. If you are not sure about something, ask.

- honesty and integrity. This is the ability to avoid dishonest actions, such as lying or stealing. Take care of employer's tools and equipment, and be accountable. Always do what you say you will do.

- initiative or self-motivation. Do things without being told. Always look for things that need to be done and assist others in need. Also look for new skills to learn.

- organization. Learn to be organized. Keep things clean, neat, and in their place. This will also help you to be more productive.

- personal phones. Keep your cell phones in your purse, pocket, desk drawer, locker, or out of view as much as possible. Be sensitive to your employer's expectations on this matter. Sometimes it is okay to have them out or charged, but don't make a habit of it. Sometimes cell phones are allowed for work, but when they are not, be mindful because someone may be watching. Way too many people are addicted to their cell phones when they do not have to be. Same situation in cars. They continue to be a major distraction. It is all about self-discipline like anything else.

- positive attitude. Employers look for the 3As: Attitude, Attitude, Attitude. Always try to look at situations in a positive rather than a negative way. Think about what is right and good instead of what is wrong and bad. Speak about what can be done instead of what cannot. Share good news and events, rather than complaining, and compliment others.

- productivity. An employee is expected to complete/produce a certain amount of work. The output of work is known as productivity. Try to do something productive each day. It will also give you a sense of accomplishment.

- quality work. Produce work that is done carefully, accurately, and thoroughly. Quality means how well the job is performed.

- reliability. The ability to do every task correctly and completely every time. Also to be there and on time.

- respect. To have consideration or concern for another person and yourself. Everyone comes from different backgrounds; therefore, it is important to respect their work, ideas, personalities, and backgrounds. Address people with Mr. Miss, Mrs. Sir, or Ma'am.

- team player. The ability to work well with others to achieve any common goal. Ask others if they need assistance. Someday they will come to your rescue.

- time-management skills. These have a great deal to do with work ethics. You need to be organized, focused, disciplined, multitask oriented, learn to say no, and be a "now" person! We all need to manage ourselves.

Employer Feedback

Comments from Local Businesses on Applicants and Employees

Do you want to obtain a job and or keep it? Here are some tips on what to do and what not do.

Several students and adults have lost their jobs because they did not show up for work or call-in to notify the employer. Others have lost their jobs because they had friends come in and spend too much time visiting or their friends stole merchandise.

Following are some reasons why applicants lost their jobs before they started:

- not being able to fill out applications, including those online
- not dressing appropriately when applying for a job or to an interview; asking for an application while shopping or dining and not appropriately dressed
- coming in pairs or groups to apply
- bringing their kids with them
- not having a social security card or ID
- simply not showing up for the interview

Following are some reasons why students and adults lost their jobs due to poor work ethic:

- not returning from break or lunch
- excessive tardiness and not being dependable
- stealing and lack of respect
- sexual harassment
- too much socializing on the new job
- not calling in when they will be late or absent
- poor customer service
- standing around and not showing initiative
- talking back to the employer and rudeness
- not following instructions
- poor dress or not following the dress code
- poor attitude and listening skills
- not being a team player
- no enthusiasm for the job or smiling
- not motivated
- can't read, write, or count
- can't read a tape measure
- dishonesty
- not taking care of company tools or equipment

- not following safety rules or procedures
- lack of social skills
- just not showing up or quitting
- using their cell phones (this includes checking the time)

One hotel manager said that if he sees applicants who are waiting for their interview using their cell phones, they usually won't be hired.

An Employer's Perspective

James G. Cole / Media / Producer (Printed with permission)

The Important characteristics I look for in an individual for hire are as follows:

1. Integrity: Be honest. When things don't go well on the job, and we all have bad days, don't make excuses or try to cover up mistakes. Learn from the experience, express concern, and relate what should have been done.
2. Attitude: Without a positive attitude on the job training is next to impossible. One must be willing to learn, take notes when being trained and be willing to work hard while maintaining a positive attitude. Accept new challenges eagerly and follow through with a given task in a timely manner.
3. Attendance: Being punctual is also being reliable. An employer must be confident that an employee will be on time whether it be for work, a client meeting or to open or close the business. It is inconsiderate when others count on you and you're late, which will often create a compromising situation for those relying on your presence.
4. Appearance: Having a neat and clean appearance is important. Clean attire, groomed hair, and appropriate jewelry are monitored by many professional organizations, therefore it is important to look neat and clean.
5. Productivity: When given a task it is important your manager knows it will get done as directed and will be done on time.
6. Organizational Skills: Being organized on the job makes a great impression, it will usually make your work less stressful, at the same time making the workload easier to handle. Be observant and make constructive suggestions when you think there may be a better way to complete the task. Your ideas may not always get implemented but over time you may find it puts you in favor with management.
7. Communication: If you want to advance with the organization you're working for, effective communication is essential. You will, "Enhance your value to your employer by keeping your manager informed about the progress of tasks." By keeping those in your organization informed you save the firm time, money, and you will earn the respect from your manager, giving yourself an advantage when promotion is considered.
8. Teamwork: Working well with others is important to the work place structure. Most jobs require individuals to work together to accomplish common goals for the good of the company. If you cannot work well with others to project deadlines the job quality could be compromised. This is a disadvantage for everyone on a team. Cooperation is key for the success of any team and as a result it will benefit the individual.

Thank you, Mr. Cole, for your valuable input!

Following are short comments from Debbie Picalo, retail chain personnel manager:

(Printed By Permission)

APPLICATIONS: Paper applications, keep them neat an accurate.

Computer applications: make sure you allow yourself enough time to complete all areas. If possible, complete it in a quiet area.

INTERVIEWS: Be prepared, bring a pen, resume, turn off cell phones and bring two forms of ID. Your social **security** card and a valid picture ID.

Dress to impress. "I have turned away applicants because of the way they were dressed."

Cell Phones: "If cell phone rings during the interview, I have stopped the interview and sent the applicant home."

WORK PLACE: Appearance, always follow company guidelines for attire. Clean, neat, not too tight, short or baggy. Remember you are the ambassador for your company and might be the only employee that the customer sees. Always make a good impression.

MY PET PEEVES: Cell phones. They have no place at the work place. Unless approved by your employer. Appearance, Follow the dress code; do not dress as if you were hanging with your friends. This is YOUR JOB, Remember that there is always someone looking for a job, maybe yours.

Thank you, Debbie Picalo, for your valuable input!

The Three D's To Motivation

DETERMINATION

DRIVE

DEDICATION

T.E.A.M.

TEACH

    ENFORCE

        ADVOCATE

           MODEL

= EFFECTIVE

    CHARACTER

      BUILDING

"Team work makes the dream work" _ John Maxwell

TEAM BUILDING

(Anonymous & revised)

Team: an energetic group of people who are committed to achieving common objectives, who work well together and enjoy doing so, and who produce high-quality results.

Following are the attributes of team players:

- goal oriented with purpose
- share responsibility
- effective communication
- conflict resolution
- creativity
- leadership
- integrity
- positive attitude and team spirit

Teamwork. A dependency is a relationship in which people count on one another. People depend on one another in work situations. The success of a company can depend upon the contribution of every team member of the employee's team. If one worker lets down the other coworkers or the company, it may cause job loss. Each person on a team depends on the contribution of other workers. All workers as a whole are more important than one single person. As a worker, you are doing a job that adds to the performance of the other workers.

There is no "I" in team.

"People Acting Together as a Group Can Accomplish Things. Which No Individual Acting Alone Could Ever Hope to Bring About."

—Franklin Delano Roosevelt

Time Management

Has a great deal to do with work ethics!

Everyone has **twenty-four** hours in a day and **seven** days in a week. How you spend your time is up to you. **T**o have good time-management skills**,** it is essential that you make good use of your time and learn to set priorities.

Everyone is busy doing something or busy doing nothing. People always say, "I am too busy" or "I don't have time." Truly, we all make time for what we want to do!

If you want to have great time-management skills, you need to be organized, focused, disciplined, multitask oriented, learn to say no, and be a "now" person.

Thomas Edison said, "There is time for everything."

"I have time for whatever I need to make time for."
Robin L. Rask

Manage yourself not your time

Many of us claim our days are never wasted. "I'm very organized," we say. "I know where I am going and what I'm going to do." If you truly feel that way, you may be in the minority. Most people become frustrated with a day that is unproductive. We would all like to get more done in a day.

The idea of time management has been in existence for more than one hundred years. Unfortunately, the term *time management* creates a false impression about what a person is able to do. Time can't be managed; time is uncontrollable. We can only manage ourselves and our use of time.

Time management is actually self-management. It's interesting that the skills we need to manage others are usually the same skills we need to manage ourselves, such as, the ability to plan, delegate, organize, direct, control, and focus.

There are common time wasters, which need to be identified. In order for a time-management process to work, it is important to know what aspects of our personal management need to be improved. Some employees who are observant can see all kinds of things that employers/bosses may ignore. Next time you are at work, look around at your fellow workers for a day/week and see how their normal routine is throughout the day. Same applies to school. It could surprise you. Or not!

Following are some of the most frequent reasons for reducing effectiveness in the workplace. Identify your time stealers.

- ☐ interruptions—telephone, visitors
- ☐ meetings
- ☐ tasks you should have delegated
- ☐ procrastination and indecision
- ☐ acting without complete information
- ☐ dealing with team members
- ☐ crisis management (firefighting)
- ☐ unclear communication
- ☐ inadequate technical knowledge
- ☐ unclear objectives and priorities

- ☐ lack of planning
- ☐ stress and fatigue
- ☐ inability to say no
- ☐ desk management and personal disorganization

Fortunately, there are strategies you can use to manage your time, be more in control, and reduce stress. You can analyze your time and see how you may be both the cause and the solution to your time challenges.

Following are time-management issues in more detail:

1. Shifting priorities and crisis management. Management guru Peter Drucker says, "Crisis management is actually the form of management preferred by most managers." The irony is that actions taken prior to the crisis could have prevented the fire in the first place.

2. The telephone. Have you ever had one of those days when you thought your true calling was telemarketing? The telephone, our greatest communication tool, can be our biggest enemy to effectiveness if we don't know how to control its hold over us. Try using e-mail whenever possible, especially with those you know like to talk and talk …

3. Texting. How many of us have difficulty staying away from our devices? If you know people who always respond immediately when you text them, they are the ones addicted to their devices. The good news is, if you need an urgent response, you can usually count on them! Many of them steal time from the employer, the ones they are with, and themselves. We could *all* learn to be more sensitive to this issue. Before cell phones were invented, people actually ate a whole meal at the table and discussed their day without an electronic device and survived just fine. Yes, change is good and often needed, but it is not always for the better.

4. Lack of priorities and objectives. This probably is the biggest, most important time waster. It affects all we do both professionally and personally. Those who accomplish the most in a day know exactly what they want to accomplish. Unfortunately, too many of us think that goals and objectives are yearly things, not daily considerations. This results in too much time spent on the minor things and not on the things that are important to our work and lives.

5. Attempting too much. Many people today feel they have to accomplish everything yesterday and don't give themselves enough time to do things properly. This leads to half-finished projects and no feeling of achievement. It is awesome when you

can leave work at the end of the day and say, "Thank you, God, for allowing me to be productive today and to make a difference."

6. Drop-in visitors. The five deadliest words that rob your time are "Have you got a minute?" Everyone is the culprit—colleagues, the boss, your peers, even friends. Knowing how to deal with interruptions is one of the best skills you can learn. Often you need to just apologize and tell them you need to get back to your work.

7. Talkers. If some of your coworkers are chatterboxes, you will need to decide when and if to talk to them or better to send them an e-mail. If they are talking too much, just kindly excuse yourself so you won't lose thirty to sixty minutes. This can also happen in your personal life with your family and friends. It may be better to talk to them when you have more time. Or learn to end the conversation or visit in a kind and timely manner.

8. Ineffective delegation. Good delegation is considered a key skill in both managers and leaders. The best managers have an ability to delegate work to staff and ensure it is done correctly. This is probably the best way of building a team's morale and reducing your workload at the same time. The general rule is this: If one of your staff can do it 80 percent as well as you can, delegate it. However, make sure not to overload them. But if you do, they can delegate one of their other responsibilities to someone else. That could be a win-win!

9. The cluttered desk. When you have finished reading this, look at your desk. If you can see less than 80 percent of it, you are probably suffering from "desk stress." The most effective people work from clear and organized desks. Sometimes you need to put things in piles and label them. Don't pile stuff on top of stuff; try to keep everything organized as much as possible, at home and in your car. It takes more effort to be unorganized than not. Organization starts at home, then at school, then to the workplace. And makes you look good!

10. Procrastination. The biggest thief of time is not decision making but decision avoidance. "Should I go or should I stay?" Often people in relationships ponder this for way too long. If that's not a time stealer! Lol! By reducing the amount of procrastinating, you can substantially increase the amount of active time available to you.

11. The inability to say no. The general rule is if people can dump their work or problems onto your shoulders, they will do it. Some of the most stressed people around lack the skill to "just say no" for fear of upsetting people. The same is true with your personal life. Sometimes you need to tell your friends, "Sorry, I cannot

go with you because I have other priorities and/or commitments at this time." They should understand.

12. Meetings. Studies have shown that the average manager spends about seventeen hours a week in meetings, about six hours in planning time, and untold hours in the follow-up. It is widely acknowledged that about as much of a third of the time spent in meetings is wasted due to poor meeting management and lack of planning.

Following are some strategies you can use to manage your time:

☐ **Always define your objectives as clearly as possible.** Do you find you are not doing what you want because you have not set goals? One of the factors that mark successful people is their ability to work out what they want to achieve and have written goals that they can review constantly. Your long-term goals should impact your daily activities and be included in your "to do" list. Without a goal or objective, people tend to just drift personally and professionally.

☐ **Analyze your use of time.** Are you spending enough time on the projects that, although may not be urgent now, you need to do to develop yourself or your career? If you are constantly asking yourself, "What is the most important use of my time right now?" it will help you to focus on important tasks and stop reacting to tasks that seem urgent (or pleasant) but carry no importance toward your goals.

☐ **Have a plan.** How can you achieve your goals without a plan? Most people know what they want but have no plan to achieve it except by sheer hard work. Your yearly plan should be reviewed regularly and reset as your achievements are met. Successful people make lists constantly. It enables them to stay on top of priorities and enables them to remain flexible to changing priorities. This should be done for both personal and business goals. You can keep a notepad at your workstation and at home. In addition, you can have a magnet erase board on your refrigerator for reminders, posters, or whatever works best for you.

☐ **Action plan for surprises.** Problems will always occur. The value of a good plan is to identify problems early and seek out solutions. Good time management enables you to measure the progress toward your goals because what you can measure, you can control. Always try to be proactive.

Unless you are committed to building time-management techniques into your daily routine, you may only achieve partial (or no) results and then make comments like "I tried time management once, and it doesn't work for me." (This is like a diet analogy.) Managing your time is much easier than going on a diet and trying to lose weight.

The more time we spend planning our time and activities, the more time we will have for those activities. By setting goals and eliminating time wasters, and doing this every day, we will find extra time to spend on those people and activities that are most important to us.

Instructions for Time-Management Chart

Great classroom activity!

Write down everything you do for a week in half-hour and one-hour increments. At the end of each day, total the hours you think were wasted or unproductive. Then add the total for the week.

This will tell you how you spend your 168 hours of the week.

Remember—be a "now" person and learn to say no! Put your money where your time is!

We all make time for what we want to do.

"Remember that time is money."
—Benjamin Franklin

	Sunday	Monday	Tuesday	Wednesday	Thursday	Friday	Saturday
		Time Management					
12:00am							
12:30am							
1:00am							
1:30am							
2:00am							
2:30am							
3:00am							
3:30am							
4:00am							
4:30am							
5:00am							
5:30am							
6:00am							
6:30am							
7:00am							
7:30am							
8:00am							
8:30am							
9:00am							
9:30am							
10:00am							
10:30am							
11:00am							
11:30am							
Wasted AM Hours							
Total Wasted Hours							

Time Management

	Sunday	Monday	Tuesday	Wednesday	Thursday	Friday	Saturday
12:00pm							
12:30pm							
1:00pm							
1:30pm							
2:00pm							
2:30pm							
3:00pm							
3:30pm							
4:00pm							
4:30pm							
5:00pm							
5:30pm							
6:00pm							
6:30pm							
7:00pm							
7:30pm							
8:00pm							
8:30pm							
9:00pm							
9:30pm							
10:00pm							
10:30pm							
11:00pm							
11:30pm							
Wasted PM Hours							
Total Wasted Hours							

Stress and Burnout

If constant stress has you feeling physically, mentally, and emotionally exhausted, you may be suffering from burnout. It is critical to recognize the symptoms. We all have stress sometimes due to jobs, finances, spouses, kids, deaths, health issues, etc. And we all deal with it in different ways. We need to know what our limits are.

Sometimes, we just need to go outside to breathe some fresh air. Other times we need a break, vacation, change of scenery, someone to talk to, or to see a doctor. Often we need to change our normal way of doing things, such as exercising and eating better. Some may seek spiritual paths, and sometimes we have to change jobs. It takes a unique person to do every job. We need to be in a job that lets us use our God-given talents.

Most things become routine after awhile. You may be burned out and fatigued by your lifestyle. This may be the time to do some soul-searching and analyze what can be changed. I find it helpful to get out of town, go to the beach, or work in the yard, which is very therapeutic for me, to clear my head. Sometimes we may get into a rut where we keep doing the same thing day after day. It's possible that you may be burned out in a relationship or marriage. If that is the case, it might be wise to spice up that part of your life or move on. Most of the time life is just Monday, Tuesday, Wednesday, Thursday, Friday, Saturday, Sunday … Get up, go to work, come home, clean, run the kids around, cook, go to bed, and get up the next day and do it all over again.

Whether you work full time or are home all day raising kids, there may be times when you reach overload. If you are a stay-at-home mom, when your husband comes home from work, show him you care. Ask about his day. Then later you can share your day and challenges with him. Allow your spouse some time to unwind from a hectic day. For some who come home from work, sitting in your car to relax for a while might be very helpful. Being a single parent can cause a great deal of stress, too, since there is no spouse to help share the responsibilities.

Debts and bills can cause major stress. When we go shopping or buy a new car, we need to ask ourselves if we really need this and if we can afford it. Will we be happy with this tomorrow, next week, or next month? When we make a purchase, it is wise to ask ourselves if this is wisdom and if we have peace about it.

Life today is generally stressful and demanding, certainly in America. When I visit family in Europe, I always admire how laid-back everyone is. They are less in a hurry and spend more time with family and friends. They make time to have meals together and afternoon tea with cake. Most of the businesses are also closed on Sundays.

Stress can be a silent mental enemy. Signs of stress typically include tiredness, chronic fatigue, uncertainty or worry, forgetfulness, a sense of helplessness, never having a sense of accomplishment, or feeling like a failure, just to name a few.

Since stress is a common factor in many illnesses, it is wise to be on guard for symptoms like headaches, migraines, tension, high blood pressure, or heart disease. Maybe if we can deal with the fruit of our problems, we will be able to deal with the roots. In the Bible it says, "Let not your hearts be troubled."

Burnout is a state of emotional and physical exhaustion caused by excessive and prolonged stress. It can occur when you feel overwhelmed and unable to meet constant demands or deadlines. When you start feeling stressed or burned out, recognize it and change some things as soon as possible. We all need peace and balance in our lives.

If your job causes you stress but you cannot or do not want to leave, speak with your boss about some alternatives, such as

- a transfer to another office or department
- new duties or fewer responsibilities
- additional help
- some cross training
- attending seminars and professional growth conferences
- taking time off or a leave of absence
- taking some new classes
- offering suggestions about the skills you have and how you can better help the company
- volunteering for a committee

We all have skills, gifts, and talents and often are not using them in our workplaces. It has been said, "Every problem has a solution and a purpose."

Dr. Don Colbert has written some excellent books on health describing what foods to eat and what to avoid by using biblical principles. What we eat and do not eat can have a huge impact on our health and moods. We are encouraged to drink a lot of water each day and eat fresh fruits and vegetables. We are also encouraged to limit our red meat intake, include whole grain wheat products, and get at least eight hours of sleep each night. I take a bottle of water with me almost everywhere I go. Many have stated that fasting one day each week is great cleansing for our body, mind, and spirit.

As studies have demonstrated, stocking up on carbohydrates like potatoes and pasta can help reduce stress and promote healthier living. Pasta provides energy, protein, and vitamin

B and promotes a feeling of calmness by boosting serotonin levels. Sometimes I eat a baked potato for lunch, which is rich in vitamin C and contains potassium. It is also filling.

When we are under stress, we should avoid consuming alcohol or sugary foods. This will lead to vitamin B depletion, which can lead to loss of memory and depression. Walking and cycling can further reduce your stress levels. Green apples and the scent of lavender have been shown to have therapeutic value. Research supported by the American Massage Therapy Association has shown that foot massage lowers levels of stress hormones. I used to give my ex-husband foot and back massages regularly.

In addition, how often have we been reminded, "An apple a day helps keep the doctor away"? Many doctors are prescribing laughter as a miracle drug. Some findings have demonstrated that laughter causes an increase in the activity of natural cells that attack and kill tumor cells and viruses. Therefore, you may want to stock up on some funny movies and start laughing. Perhaps it might be more a case of "A laugh a day keeps the doctor away."

A few tips by Don Colbert, M.D.

- Fatty fish, such as mackerel, salmon, herring, sardines, and tuna, are rich sources of DHA, which is a fish oil that helps to create healthier brain cells.
- The healthiest nuts for the brain are walnuts, which actually look like miniature brains, and almonds.
- Foods with the greatest antioxidant capacity are the healthiest for the brain. These include fruits such as prunes, raisins, blueberries, blackberries, strawberries and raspberries. Vegetables with the highest antioxidant capacity include garlic, kale, spinach, Brussels sprouts, alfalfa sprouts, and broccoli.
- Olive oil, avocados, macadamia nuts, and other monounsaturated fats help to prevent memory loss.

Imagine life as a game in which you are juggling five balls in the air. You name them—work, family, health, friends, and spirit—and you're keeping all of these in the air. You will soon understand that work is a rubber ball. If you drop it, it will bounce back. But the other four balls—family, health, friends, and spirit are made of glass. If you drop one of these, they will be irrevocably scuffed, marked, nicked, damaged, or even shattered. They will never be the same. You must understand that and strive for balance in your life.

Bryan Dyson, CEO of Coca Cola Enterprises 1959-1964

List some things that cause you stress and then make a list of how you can reduce that stress.

Causes of My Stress:

Resolutions for My Stress:

Holiday Stress Busters

Holidays are a time for family, friends, and fun, but they can also be very stressful. Holidays can also be painful for many due to the loss of a loved one or just being alone. Following are some suggestions that may ease some stress.

Plan ahead. Many people are procrastinators and wait until the last minute for everything. Some even shop on Christmas Eve, only to fight with the crowds and the lack of merchandise. Others plan ahead; they start shopping after Christmas for sales for the next year. If you are planning on a party, start as soon as you make the decision. Little by little, every day it comes together. If you wait until the last minute, it can become very overwhelming, especially if things don't turn out the way you had planned. *Time management* is a key factor in this.

Delegate. Share the responsibilities like the shopping, cooking, cleaning, etc. Why do it all if you will only to be stressed and exhausted afterward?

Sleep. Get enough sleep so you won't be cranky and will have plenty of energy.

Overindulging. Anything you do should always be done in moderation. For example, if you hate the holidays because you always gain five pounds, make a goal to lose a few pounds before the holidays and you won't feel so guilty later.

Budget. Set a budget and stick to it! Many of us get carried away when shopping for the holidays. It is too easy to say, "Charge it!" This is how you get into debt and become stressed. Then you will end up with post-holiday blues. You don't have to buy for everyone. A lot of times we buy things that people don't like or need anyway. Put some thought into your budget and who you really need to buy for and what would be practical for them. Gift certificates or money always works. If you are on a limited budget, there are creative ways to buy or do things. Buy things during the year, one at a time, on sale. When you get gifts you don't like or need, put them in a box and be a blessing to someone else. (Some call this re gifting.)

Change. Put your spare loose change in a bottle every day. You will be surprised how it adds up!

Stressed spelled backward is *desserts*!

How to Make New Year's Resolutions Stick

Many of us start out the New Year wanting to make changes, achieve goals, lose weight, etc. Before we know it, the next year is upon us and nothing has changed. Sound familiar? Here are some suggestions.

First of all, nothing will happen unless you make a decision.

Change has to come from within. Nothing happens on the outside unless it first starts on the inside. Don't try to change everything at once; Rome was not built in a day. Make small changes, one or two things at a time. And be realistic. Some people do not like change; however, change is inevitable. (Except from a vending machine.)

Be specific. If you want to lose weight, how much? If you want money in the bank, how much? If you want to get a job, how bad and by when? Take baby steps toward your goals.

Set a deadline. "As soon as possible" is not realistic. Deadlines, as we know, are commitments and have certain timelines.

Consistency is the key to all victory!

Coping with Anxiety and Stress

The following six activities will help you become aware of how you would handle yourself in these anxiety-provoking and stressful situations:

A. Your boss just told you that if you came in late one more time you would be fired. How will you respond?

B. Your parent has just informed you he or she cannot take you to work this morning. What will you do?

C. You work in a fast food restaurant. The person who works the drive-up window calls in sick. Your boss tells you to work the window, but you have never worked that position before. It is lunchtime. What will you do?

Responsibility for Your Own Behavior

A. You are going to an interview and you accidentally get caught in a water sprinkler. What will you do?

B. You are a delivery person for a local flower shop. Due to a traffic violation, your license has been suspended for thirty days. How will you explain this to your employer?

C. You are working in a customer service area. An irate customer approaches you with a problem. You respond to her rudeness with a sarcastic comment. She threatens to discuss your behavior with your supervisor. What will you do?

Example

Letter of Resignation

Date

Ms. Robin Rask, Manager
Diamond's Restaurant
7777 Diamond Drive
Sun Valley, CA 90707

Dear Ms. Rask:

Please accept my resignation from my job as a cashier. My last day of work will be April 15, 2017. I will be accepting a position with more work hours.

I appreciate the wonderful experience and training I have had at Diamond's Restaurant. I have learned many valuable job skill tools while working with you. I will be more than happy to train my replacement. Thank you for accepting my resignation.

Sincerely,

MaryAnn Needy

MaryAnn Needy

LEAVING YOUR JOB?

When terminating a job, you need to make sure you will have a positive reference for your future job!!

- Don't just quit, Calm down, and think it over.
- Complete all job responsibilities.
- Offer to train their new employee.
- Make sure you have another job before you quit.
- Give a verbal or written notice to your employer FIRST.
- Complete all job responsibilities.
- Offer to train a new employee.
- Ask for a letter of reference or recommendation.
- Don't bad mouth your employer.
- Don't brag about your new job to other employees.
- Offer to be available later for phone questions.

- Do leave with good feelings.

Recreated and printed with permission, Partners & Education/Youth Programs/Poway Unified School District.

The ABCs of Loving Your Job

I've discovered that loving the job you have, or finding a job you can love, is dependent on three things. Dr. John C. Maxwell calls these "The ABCs of loving your job."

(Printed with permission by Dr. John C. Maxwell)

ASSOCIATES: Work with people you enjoy.

For years I have bragged about my staff. I realize that not everyone is surrounded with my kind of staff. The good news is you can develop one. When I talk to leaders about hiring people, I advise them to hire first for *affinity*, second for *character*, and third for *specific skills*. If you bring on someone you like whom you can trust, you can teach him or her whatever skills they needs for the job.

Regarding your existing staff, don't forget that people skills can be learned as well. If you are willing to make the investment, you can cultivate the right kind of people that everyone wants to be around.

BELIEF: Trust that your work is worthwhile and making a vital difference.

Bob Buford has written that many people spend the first half of their career pursuing success. When success alone is found to be lacking, they give the second half to the pursuit of significance, which is far more satisfying.

If your job is not making a difference in this world, by all means get out there and find something else. But in many situations, you'll find a sense of making a difference through your work if you simply look for it.

CHALLENGE: Find a job big enough to let you keep growing for the rest of your life.

Like shoes that are too small pinch the feet, a job that is too small pinches a leader's spirit. If the job you have now offers no opportunity to grow, decide to grow anyway. Invest in your own personal development, sharpening leadership skills, interpersonal skills, and technical skills. What you'll discover is that your organization will find a place for a person who has made a priority out of growth. And if they don't, the competition will! And keep this in mind when you consider your top performers. Are you providing room for your top performers to grow? If you don't, someone else will.

Finding joy in your work, or evaluating a lack of joy, can be achieved by considering associates, beliefs, and challenges.

Love what you do, or do something else.

You'll never achieve real success unless you enjoy what you're doing.

No one has ever succeeded in a line of endeavor they did not like.

Your chances of success are directly proportional to the
degrees of pleasure you derive from what you do.

If you're in a job you hate, get out.

It's better to be a failure in something you love, than
attempting to be a success in something you don't.

Don't set compensation as a goal.

Find the work you love, and the compensation will follow.

The more you love what you are doing, the more successful it will be for you and others!

—Unknown and Revised

Ten Simple Ways to Lose Your Job

Any of the following will lead to your dismissal with an employer:

- stealing. This means even a pencil or pen or time.

- poor customer service. You need to treat the customers well. Always communicate in a positive way and remember your body talks, so smile.

- socializing on the job. Be sure not to focus on your friends and ignore the customers.

- dishonesty. Taking money or giving things away to your family or friends.

- not following directions. Know and follow company rules and regulations. Follow directions carefully, and take notes if necessary.

- poor work quality. Do good work. Make sure that the job and you are suited. If you don't do well, make a change.

- sexual harassment. This includes coworkers and customers alike, off-color jokes, inappropriate touching or comments, pushing for a date, etc.

- tardiness. Be on time to work at the start of your shift and also when returning from breaks and lunch.

- undependability. This makes you unreliable, and if they can't count on you being there, there is no point in expecting you.

- lack of respect. You must respect your boss, coworkers, and customers.

Getting to Know the Job

Your First Day at Work

The first day on the job is difficult for everyone, similar to the first day of school. It's common for new workers to feel unsure of themselves, to make mistakes, and to forget names. Some even get lost! But most people manage to get through it all right. During the first couple of weeks on the job, the worker learns job duties and gets to know the other employees. Most employers expect workers to have some problems during the breaking-in period. That's why so many large companies put their new employees through special training or orientation programs to introduce them to the company and to their new job.

At some businesses, the older workers put new employees through their own kind of orientation. They may tease them, ask them for tools that don't exist, or send the new employees on errands. This is often called "gopher work" because the new worker is asked to "go for" this and "go for" that. This will show the employer some of your work ethics. The new employee just needs to keep a sense of humor and remember that this won't last very long. If it does, you may want to look for a new job.

Most of the time, the boss and the other workers are eager to help the new employee learn the job and join the regular work crew. The sooner the trainee learns the job, the better it is for everyone. After you have been there for a few weeks, ask for feedback on your performance.

Pay Attention to the Following:

Appearance, Grooming, and Dress

First impressions are lasting impressions! Look in the mirror! Men, please keep your pants pulled up. If you were the employer, would you hire you?

Body Care

These seven rituals are a must!

1. Shower or bathe daily. You'll look better, smell good, and feel better. Cologne can be used, but be sure it is not overpowering.

2. Take care of your hair. Shampoo it regularly. Keep it combed and brushed. Never, never allow dandruff to mar your appearance.

3. Use makeup sparingly. Apply it carefully to emphasize your best features. War paint is out. You want to influence, not conquer!

4. Shave as often as necessary if you're a man. Twice daily, if you must. There is no excuse for a five-o'clock shadow. It doesn't make you look macho; it only makes you look unshaven! Use good aftershave.

5. Brush your teeth. Sometimes you may need to also use mouthwash. Always make sure to have fresh breath.

6. Keep nails clean and trimmed. If you're a man, a manicure is a matter of personal choice. If you're a woman, choose a nail polish that complements your hands, not one that calls undue attention to them. Make sure your polish is all the way on or all the way off.

7. Check your posture. Stand tall. Hold yourself erect, shoulders back, belly in. (Remember what Mom taught you!)

Getting Along on the Job

Getting along on the job is not difficult. Here are some hints to help you be successful once you have your job.

1. Find out how you are doing. If your supervisor doesn't meet with you regularly to evaluate your progress, you should ask him or her how you are doing. You should find out what things your supervisor thinks you do well and what things need to be done better. Then you will know what parts of your job need extra effort and you will catch problems before they become big deals. If your supervisor says you need to do better at something, politely ask him or her to show you how to do it better. This is extremely important if you are in a training program or internship and expect to be hired!

2. Ask questions and listen carefully. Be sure that you know what your duties are and how to do them right. When you are being trained or given instructions, listen very carefully and ask as many questions as you need to. Don't be afraid to say, "I don't understand," or "Please show me how again," or "I forgot." Write things down if you cannot remember. Always ask for help when you need it, and follow safety rules. Be sure you know what you are doing before you start a task.

3. Keep busy. If you find that you have run out of work, don't sit or stand around waiting for somebody to tell you what to do next. Look around to see what still needs to be done. If you don't see anything, go to your supervisor and ask for more work. This is called taking initiative.

4. Take care of your personal appearance. Wear clothing that is right for the job and try to cover tattoos. Keep your pants pulled up. Get enough sleep so you look alert.

5. Always do your best. Everyone is different. If you can work really fast and still get the job done right, that's great! It is okay if you are steady and reliable too. Just make sure that you are doing your best, even if others are goofing off or socializing. You may not enjoy every part of your job, but that is life.

6. Show enthusiasm and good work ethics. Have a positive attitude, use good judgment, and show that you enjoy your job. Ask for new challenges. Learn to manage your time wisely. Stay off your cell phone and avoid gossip. Do what you say you will do. This is called integrity. Some Bs to keep in mind are:

   - be courteous and prompt,
   - be a team player,

- be a self-starter,
- be creative,
- be honest and loyal,
- be confident,
- be committed,
- be organized and productive,
- be a problem solver, and
- be adaptable.

7. Customer service. Greet customers promptly with a smile. Treat customers as guests. Apologize when needed and go the extra mile.

8. Schedules. Be dependable, responsible, and reliable. Write down your work schedule, and keep track of your hours and days worked on your calendar. Make sure you call your employer in advance if you might be late, are ill or need time off. If you have to quit your job, make sure to give employer two-weeks notice whenever possible.

Qualities of a Leader

"A great leader's courage to fulfill his vision comes from passion, not position."

—John Maxwell

All effective leaders have the following twenty qualities:

1. A leader is always full of praise.

2. A leader learns to use the phrases "thank you" and "please" on his way to the top.

3. A leader is always growing.

4. A leader is possessed with his dreams.

5. A leader launches forth before success is certain.

6. A leader is not afraid of confrontation.

7. A leader talks about his own mistakes before talking about someone else's.

8. A leader is a person of honesty and integrity.

9. A leader has a good name.

10. A leader makes others better.

11. A leader is quick to praise and encourages the smallest amount of improvement.

12. A leader is genuinely interested in others.

13. A leader looks for opportunities to find someone doing something right.

14. A leader responds to his own failures and acknowledges them before others have to discover and reveal them.

15. A leader is specific in what he expects.

16. A leader takes others up with him.

17.   A leader never allows murmuring from himself or others.

18.   A leader holds accountable those who work with him.

19.   A leader does what is right rather than what is popular.

20.   A leader is a servant and leads by example.

(Anonymous)

America's Drug Problem

God bless mothers who drug us!

The other day, someone at a store in our town read that a methamphetamine lab had been found in an old farmhouse in the adjoining county and he asked me a rhetorical question,

"Why didn't we have a drug problem when you and I were growing up?"

I replied: I had a drug problem when I was young:

I was drug to church on Sunday morning.

I was drug to church for weddings and funerals.

I was drug to family reunions and community socials no matter the weather.

I was drug by my ears when I was disrespectful to adults.

I was also drug to the woodshed when I disobeyed my parents, told a lie, brought home a bad report card, did not speak with respect, spoke ill of the teacher or preacher, or if I didn't put forth my best effort in everything that was asked of me.

I was drug to the kitchen sink to have my mouth washed out with soap

if I uttered a profane four-letter word.

I was drug out to pull weeds in Mom's garden and flowerbeds

and cockleburs out of Dad's fields.

I was drug to the homes of family, friends, and neighbors to help out some poor soul who had no one to mow the yard, repair the clothesline, or chop some firewood, and if my mother had ever known that I took a single dime as a tip for this kindness, she would have drug me back to the woodshed.

Those drugs are still in my veins; and they affect my behavior in everything I do, say, and think. They are stronger than cocaine, crack, or heroin; and if today's children had this kind of drug problem, *America would be a better place.*

—Anonymous

Chapter 5

Customer Service

In *business*, **U** comes

before **I**

bUsIness

Providing Excellent Customer Service

Do the following to provide excellent customer service:

- Smile in person and on the telephone.
- Use appropriate greeting when answering the telephone.
- Say, "How may I help or serve you today?"
- Try to use the customer's name.
- Listen and take notes.
- Listen to the customer's concern.
- Replace "I'm sorry" with "I apologize."
- Empathize, make eye contact, be patient, and stop talking.
- Check your emotions, remove distractions, and ask open questions.
- Paraphrase back to the customer what you heard him or her say.
- Be genuine and sincere. Use customer-sensitive language.
- Customers are looking to *you* to help with their concerns.
- Do not promise the customer what you cannot deliver.
- Follow up with your customers.
- Put yourself in the customer's shoes. Be friendly.
- Always treat customers like you would want to be treated.
- Remember you are a customer too.
- Give professional care to ALL your customers.
- Create a welcoming environment. Make customers feel at home.
- Make teamwork work. Involve all staff in continuous improvement.
- Take initiative, ask for help, and go the extra mile.
- Personally direct customers to where they need to go.
- Award staff for jobs well done.
- Always treat customers as guests and with dignity and respect.

Use the First Thirty Seconds

"When you first encounter a customer, a good relationship with him or her is almost always less than thirty seconds away … you can practically ensure this good relationship just by making simple changes in three specific areas: your opening greeting, your first response, and your ability to actively listen to people."

—Richard S. Gallagher, Great Customer Connections

Customer Complaints

All customer complaints are serious, especially when the customer is upset.

Customers want attention, courtesy, respect, and a resolution in a timely manner. Never ignore or make light of a customer complaint. Do not try to figure out who is to blame. Customers do not care that you are short staffed, have computer issues, or anything else. When faced with a complaint, do the following:

- Always apologize first.
- Listen to make sure you understand the issue. Don't interrupt. Sometimes they just need to vent, which helps calm them down.
- Show the customer you care.
- Ask questions.
- Do not tolerate abuse or threats.
- Work with the customer to resolve the problem.
- Try to take care of the problem quickly.
- If you cannot help the customer, find someone who can.
- Have integrity. Do what you say you will do.
- Be a problem solver.
- Follow up with the customer when needed.
- Provide them with a discount or other free service.

If you do not provide great customer service, they will not come back and will tell all their other friends about you and your service. All business thrives on repeat customers.

We as customers have different expectations of different kinds of businesses. Let's take the bank, post office, and grocery stores as an example. How many times are we standing in those long lines when there are seven-plus checkout stands and only three or four open? Who is responsible? How many times have you made a phone call, trying to speak to someone, only to get directed to another number and never get to speak to a human? Where lies the monotony in all of this?

Customer Service in the High Desert

What Is Customer Service and How Important Is It?

by

Michael Stevens, Author, *Make Sure Your Shirt Has Buttons*

(Printed with permission)

I by no means consider myself an expert on customer service, but having been in the workforce since 1968, I believe I have acquired enough experiences to write about this subject. As consumers, you and I have the right to demand and expect superior service.

What do we mean by customer service? There is no universally accepted definition. Even if a person is treated poorly, as long as he or she is served, in a technical sense that is customer service. Therefore many companies can legitimately promote the fact that they are concerned about customer service.

Customer service is more than just whether a service was rendered. It is also how it was rendered, when rendered, and the attitude, of the person giving the service. I went to a fast food restaurant and part of my order was a large orange juice. When it was delivered, most of the juice was frozen. I took the juice back and asked the clerk to please exchange it for some not frozen. She served me. But, she made me wait, acted as if she didn't want to do it, and she had the most evil look on her face as she did so. Was that customer service? She may have thought so because I got what I wanted. I say no, because she was in no hurry to accommodate me, and acted as if I was troubling her. Not once did she smile, not once did she apologize.

I define customer service as treating customers with respect and dignity at all times, trying to determine the best and most equitable way of giving the customer what he or she is seeking, and trying to view the situation from the perspective of the customer. Customer service means being honest, fair and giving the customer no less than 100% of staff's efforts. Is this too lofty a definition? I don't think so. Is it realistic? Absolutely. I realize from my own experience that there may be portions of the definition that may be difficult to perform at all times. For example, it may not be necessary to view the situation from the perspective of the customer. What would it prove? If I can't do something for a customer for whatever reason, what does it matter that I see their request from their perspective? It does matter, because it allows me to be empathetic, and therefore, more willing to do the other part of the definition, namely "to determine the best and most equitable way of giving the customer what he wants."

So, perhaps you can begin to see just how complex this issue of customer service can be. It sometimes becomes a matter of perception.

It is quite possible that a person could be in top form, providing what he or she believes to be excellent service, only to discover that the recipient is dissatisfied, or angry. How could this be? Somewhere along the line "wires get crossed." If I walked into ABC Company, I should not have to communicate to their personnel that I expect to be treated fairly and with respect. That is what I call an "unspoken" expectation.

Whoever I may deal with at ABC Company should (hopefully) have the same unspoken expectation-to treat me fairly and with respect, and expect it in return. As long as we both have the same expectation, chances are very good that the interaction will be positive. On the other hand, if I went into ABC Company and had unreasonable expectations-whether I communicated those expectations or not-the interaction is bound to be poor. What is unreasonable? For example, that I would expect that staff would drop what they were doing just to serve me, whether they were serving someone else or not. Unreasonable would be for me to expect that I would be provided special treatment, different from what other customers receive.

Here is a scenario that happened to me and I'd like for you to evaluate whether I had unreasonable expectations, if the company gave good customer service, and what would you have done as the customer or supplier?

The door handle on my mini-van broke off. In order for me to replace it I had to take apart the inside panel of the door. After disassembling the door panel, I discovered I didn't have the proper tool to install the handle. So, near the end of the business day (to not interfere with other appointments) I went to the local dealer from whom I purchased the minivan to ask if the service personnel would install the handle for me. They didn't have to remove the panel, and probably would take less than five minutes to use a certain tool (that I didn't have) to replace the handle. The dealer said to come back the next day, and the charge would be half ($27) of their hourly rate ($54). As a loyal customer I didn't believe what I was asking deserved a charge. When I described to the service representative all that was needed he didn't care. I asked for the Service Manager and he was less sympathetic than the service rep. At no point during the conversation did he say, "let's take a look and see what we can do," or, "let's take a look and maybe we can show you how to do it." Instead, he debated me and gave analogies regarding why he would not assist me. He didn't seem to want to work with me, or even care that I would leave a dissatisfied customer. He never made an effort to find a way to accommodate my request; all he was concerned about was his position.

How could this situation have been handled differently? Did I expect too much? What would you have done if you were the employer or if you were in my position, as the customer?

Note: I eventually purchased the tool to change the door handle; it was cheaper than having the dealer do it.

What you can do as customers, or consumers to improve your chance of receiving good customer service: The strategies listed below are things you can do if you are not satisfied with the manner in which you were treated. For ease of understanding, the term supplier refers to the person(s) providing the service.

(1) Don't be intimidated. Many people don't like confrontations, believing that all confrontations are negative. Not true. Confrontations-or encounters-may be brought by negative circumstances, but the interaction doesn't have to be negative. If you patronize an establishment you have the right to receive what you went there for (within reason of course). It may be uncomfortable having to talk about your dissatisfaction with the manager or a person who may look frightening. Don't worry that there could be some retribution, if anything; you'll probably be treated better next time around because the supplier will know what you won't tolerate.

(2) Be assertive. If you don't stand up for your rights-who will? You are giving more power to the supplier if you accept shabby service, and in essence are sending a message that says: "it's ok to treat me as you do." If I were a manager or owner I'd want to know how my employees are performing. You'd probably be doing the supplier a favor because they may not be aware that their behavior or performance is unacceptable. Your informing them will give them the opportunity to redeem themselves and correct the situation.

(3) Be clear, respectful and communicate your expectations. Don't expect the supplier to read your mind to know what happened, or to assume or interpret what you want to have happen. Don't ramble, just say what you want or expect. Be respectful, and address the supplier by name or title, and avoid name-calling. Don't use profanity or resort to yelling or screaming. There's a saying that goes, "you catch more flies with honey than you can with vinegar."

(4) Try not to argue. If it appears that your first line of communication is getting you nowhere, don't argue. You may know you're right, but arguing tends to put people on the defensive and it becomes a struggle to see whose position will prevail.

(5) Seek the assistance from a supervisor or manager. Be respectful and first try to resolve the concerns at the lowest possible level. If, however, you have done this and are still dissatisfied, insist on seeing someone who has the authority to rectify the situation. Be

prepared to accept the fact that a supervisor or manager may not be readily available and you may have to wait until later in the day or the next day.

(6) Put your concerns in writing. If, after trying the above-referenced strategies and you seem to get nowhere, continue to elevate your concern. Sometimes a concern is viewed differently by someone completely removed from the actual circumstance. If you resort to writing, be sure to describe circumstances in chronological order, careful to include names, dates, times and results. Be sure to make a specific request regarding what you want to have happen. Leave a phone number that you can be reached at, and request a written reply to your letter.

(7) Be flexible, willing to compromise. There will no doubt be times where your request or your expectations simply cannot be honored. Compromising is not admitting defeat; it just creates a better circumstance for a win-win situation. There will be times, of course, when you may not want to, nor should you compromise. You'll have to be the judge of the circumstances. Sometimes when you experience inferior service, it may only be an isolated circumstance brought on by who knows what. It may foretell or expose a serious problem that needs to be brought to light. Again, you'll have to judge and decide if you want to take responsibility for correcting a bad situation or simply walk away and leave it to someone else to deal with.

The root at each of these strategies is communication. The supplier of service cannot improve substandard service if he / she is unaware. Although these strategies seem to place the burden for correction with the customer, not completely. Good customer service is a 50-50 proposition.

The strategies listed for what the supplier can do are both preventive and corrective.

(1)   Create an environment and set clear expectations, which stresses provision of quality, superior, excellent customer service. Management plays a key role in determining how employees will perform, especially employees who interact with the public (whether by phone or in person). Managers should have a written policy, display that policy, and practice the policy on a consistent basis. Remember though, customer service should also be kept in mind between employees.

(2)   Seek training / provide training. Don't assume that employees are prepared to know how to interact with the public. If no one is trained in-house to provide customer service training, send employees out or hire a consultant to provide the training. Employees will feel more confident that not only do they know the company's policy; they also have the tools and knowledge to implement the policy.

(3) Empower staff. Make staff feel like they're part of the process-and therefore the solution-by granting them the authority to make decisions to handle situations at the lowest possible level. As long as the company's expectations are clear, as long as training has been provided, suppliers should feel confident and competent to handle situations between customers.

(4) Appoint an ombudsman. Suppliers who have the resources to appoint an ombudsman can significantly improve their chances of receiving public relations dividends. The ombudsman is a person to whom the public and employees can turn to assist with problem resolution. This individual should be someone with superb people skills, one who can mediate, negotiate and facilitate, and has strong tact and diplomatic skills. The ombudsman should not be seen as someone that employees automatically or arbitrarily refer to. The ombudsman should be a last resort if front line personnel can't handle or resolve a situation.

(5) Know when and to whom to refer. In the absence of an ombudsman, employees should know who should be contacted when a situation is not easily resolved at the lowest level. Nothing is more frustrating and aggravating than to be told to see so and so or talk to so and so, who in turn has to refer to so and so and so. Informing employees about who has what responsibility and authority to handle which situations will minimize the frustration factor.

(6) Don't arbitrarily, immediately say "no," seek alternatives. Nothing infuriates me more than to encounter a supplier who is so rigid; they would never entertain the idea of trying something different. When a customer makes a request that may be out of the ordinary, or unusual, try to determine if the request has merit. Try to visualize the request from the customer's perspective. Even if the supplier seeks to explore alternative choices and has to come back to "no", he or she will be seen as trying to find the best and most equitable way of giving the customer what he or she seeks.

(7) Know how/when to compromise, when to hold firm. Some customers are unreasonable beyond belief, and have to understand that they will never get what they want. Some customers create problems for themselves either because of something they said or did, or didn't say or do. In either case, supplies can't always be expected to acquiesce to customer demands. Even when a supplier must be firm, it's best to do so with kindness and respect.

(8) Don't be argumentive. If a customer has lost control and appears angry, circumstances will worsen if the supplier engages in argument or debate. Some strategies, which might diffuse the situation, are:

- Use sir or ma'am when addressing the customer. It says, "no matter how you behave, I will treat you courteously and with respect, and I hope you will do the same."
- Get the angry customer away from other customers. Angry customers tend to "grandstand", and try to show that they'll put the supplier in his or her place. Simply ask the person, "Would you please come with me and let's discuss what happened?"
- Make the customer comfortable; offer a beverage or somewhere to sit.
- Offer a consolation. Maybe the customer couldn't get what they wanted or weren't treated like they want to be treated, offer something that will make amends without making it appear as a bribe.

(9)   Apologize. It's best to apologize, even if an allegation has been made and not confirmed. For example, if a customer complains about service received, the manager could say: "I'm sorry that you feel that way." It doesn't say that the employee was wrong or bad, but what it does say is that the manager is concerned about the customer's perception of the staff and establishment, and that their opinion is valued. It is definitely advisable to admit to and apologize for bona fide mistakes. To overlook the mistake or try to cover it up, shows a "holier than thou" attitude, and makes it appear that the supplier is superior to the customer.

(10) Solicit ideas from customers / employees. The most effective way to get employee buy-in to provide quality customer service is to allow them to have some ownership about what can be done. Employees are responsible for carrying out the policies, procedures, and values of the company. Their cooperation is obtained more easily when employee opinions are solicited. Don't solicit unless you are prepared to adopt and implement. This also holds true for customers. If you have a suggestion program, you'll be seen as a hypocrite if you only ask, and not use some of the suggestions.

(11) Reward and command. Take time to acknowledge employees for their support of the quality customer service principles. Be sure to make the acknowledgements public, either at a staff meeting or an award program or employee newsletter.

(12) (Share letters / calls with employees. Whenever letters or calls are received, let the employees know. The good letters and calls confirm that the employees are being successful in their efforts at providing good customer service, and the bad suggests that more work needs to be done. Acknowledge the employees who may have been referenced when sharing the good letters, use generic terms (an employee, an associate) when sharing the bad.

(13) Take disciplinary action for substandard performance. The form of disciplinary action can run the gamut, but employees need to believe that management is serious about its commitment to provide quality customer service. Employees unwilling or unable to support management's commitment can be trained, retrained, or dismissed.

(14) Use decoys. The best way to put to the test whether suppliers subscribe to the expectations of the company is to periodically test them. Do not use decoys without letting employees know that there is a possibility that they will be tested and tested randomly. There shouldn't have to be negative circumstances in order to try to determine how employees perform.

(15) (Follow through. When suppliers make a commitment to do or not do something-especially if what was promised was designed to correct something about by the customer-make sure there is follow through. And follow through in a timely manner. Some changes will take longer than others, but communicate to the customer an approximate (and realistic) timeframe that the commitment will be honored.

Who loses because of poor customer service? Everyone loses, the customer and supplier. The customer loses because he or she is left with a negative impression when they are the recipients of poor customer service. The supplier loses because they must now have to feel the possible effects of losing customers, developing a poor reputation.

Remember, Customer service is treating all customers with respect and dignity at all times, trying to determine the best and most equitable way of giving the customer what he or she is seeking, and trying to view the situation from the perspective of the customer. Customer service means being honest and fair, and giving the customer no less than 100% of the supplier's effort.

"Quality Customer Service. It's what we all should strive to provide, no ifs ands or buts."
—Michael Stevens

Ten Things to Remember about Customers,

the Life-Blood of Every Business

1. Customers are our reason for being.

2. Customers are feeling, thinking people—not cold statistics.

3. Customers are not nuisances or interruptions.

4. The customer's wish is our command.

5. Customers are our partners, not our competitors.

6. We are here to serve customers, not match wits with them.

7. Customers are doing us the favor, not vice versa.

8. Customers deserve the best we have to offer.

9. Customers don't need us—we need them.

10. Customers sign our paychecks.

Adapted from *Speaker's Library of Business Stories, Anecdotes and Humor* by Joe Griffin

"I Am Your Customer"

"I Am Your Customer." Satisfy my wants, add personal attention and a friendly touch, and I will become a walking advertisement for your products and services. Ignore my wants, show carelessness, inattention, and poor management, and I will simply cease to exist as far as you are concerned.

I am sophisticated, much more so than I was a few years ago. My needs are more complex. I have grown accustomed to better things. I have money to spend.

I am an egotist. I am sensitive; I am proud. My ego needs the nourishment of a friendly, personal greeting from you. It is important to me that you appreciate my business. After all, when I buy your products and services, my money is feeding you.

I am a perfectionist. I want the best I can get for the money I spend. When I criticize your food, beverage, or service and I will, to anyone who will listen, when I am dissatisfied then take heed. The source of my discontent lies in something you or the products you serve have failed to do. Find that source and eliminate it, or you will lose my business and that of my friends as well.

I am fickle. Other businessmen continually beckon to me with offers of "more" for my money. To keep my business, you must offer something better than they. "I am your customer now," but you must prove to me again and again that I have made a wise choice in selecting your store, your products, and your services above all others."

—Anonymous

Treating Customers Well

Proper Customer Treatment

Being polite to a customer is very important. Following are at least four ways to do so:

1. Use a customer's name if you know it.
2. Call a woman "miss" or "ma'am;" call a man "sir."
3. Say, "excuse me," to get the attention of a customer.
4. Find out what the customer wants to know. If you do not know the answer to a customer's question, do not just say, "I don't know." Tell the customer, "I'm sorry, I do not know, but I will find out for you."

Assisting Customers

Most customers enjoy courteous and respectful service. There are times when a specific customer may need additional assistance. Always ask, "May I help you?" Be sure to wait for an answer before assisting a customer.

Some customers who may need extra help could be senior citizens, parents with babies or small children, disabled individuals, or non-English-speaking persons.

Treating customers well is an important part of any business. Below are some suggestions to help assist customers.

Helping an Older Customer

Some older people may not see or hear as well as you do. Some are not very strong. Not all older people have these problems. You will have to pay attention to older customers to see if they need your help.

Following are some suggestions to assist a senior citizen:

1. Offer to write things down if they are hard to remember.
2. Open a door for him or her.
3. Offer to read signs and menus.
4. Talk slowly and clearly to ensure that the customer hears you.
5. Offer to carry heavy bags or packages.

Helping Those with Babies or Small Children

Fathers and mothers with babies or small children may need extra help. They have their hands full! Here are some suggestions to help you assist them:

1. Open a door for them.
2. Carry bags or packages.
3. Complete the transaction as quickly as possible.

Helping a Disabled Person

A customer on crutches, or using some other type of assistive device, may need help getting through a door or finding a place to sit in a crowded restaurant. A customer who puts crutches aside to sit down will want to have the crutches close by. Never take a customer's crutches away unless the person asks you to do so. People using wheelchairs sometimes cannot reach things—offer assistance to that person before actually doing so.

Here are some suggestions to assist disabled customers:

1. Offer to open a door for them.
2. Ask them if they would like your help to read signs and menus.
3. Talk slowly and clearly. Do not yell.
4. Offer to carry heavy bags or packages.
5. Put change carefully in the person's hand.
6. Tell the person what you are doing.

Helping Those Who Do Not Speak English

Give extra time to customers who do not speak fluent English. Be patient and do your best to understand what the customer is saying. Most people can understand more of a foreign language than they can speak.

Following are some suggestions for assisting non-English-speaking persons:

1. Speak clearly and smile.
2. Gesture when necessary.

The Angry Customer

Every person on the job runs into an angry customer once in awhile. Here are some guidelines to follow when a customer gets upset:

1. Listen to what the customer is saying.

2. Say you are sorry. Even if the problem is not your fault, you should say you are sorry that it happened.
3. Explain why the problem might have happened. When the customer knows the reason for the problem, he or she might cool off.
4. Try to solve the problem. If you are not sure you can solve the problem, go to your supervisor and ask for help.
5. Contact your boss right away if the customer is very angry.
6. Above all, stay cool yourself.

(Recreated/Printed by Permission/Partners & Education /Youth Programs, Poway Unified School District)

14 Steps to Success

(Anonymous)

BE CONFIDENT – *Successful people believe in themselves. They know their actions make a difference in their lives and the lives of others. They work at trusting themselves and others.*

BE RESPONSIBLE – Successful people choose to respond with appropriate behavior and accept the consequences of their actions. They take credit for their success and learn from their mistakes.

BE HERE – Successful people go to work regularly. Once there, they are both physically and mentally present.

BE PROMPT – Successful people are always prompt. They get to where they are going on time. Others are counting on them to be on time.

BE FRIENDLY – Successful people accept the differences of others. They build friendships by helping one another rather than hurting each other. Unsuccessful people destroy by acting or speaking out in violence.

BE POLITE – Successful people show courtesy. They acknowledge the fact that other people have helped them become successful. With that in mind, they have respect for others. For instance, politely waiting their turn.

BE PREPARED – Successful people always come prepared with their materials when expected. They keep their tools and supplies in good condition. To be prepared, a successful person must always plan ahead.

BE A LISTENER – Successful people listen to instructions and follow directions. Since they listen to what others need, they can cooperate to achieve success.

BE A WORKER – Successful people keep working. They spend their time on the things that will generate production and earnings. They will keep focused even when others get off track.

BE A TOUGH WORKER – Successful people keep trying. They keep trying towards their goals even when things get difficult.

BE A RISK TAKER – Successful people have courage and are willing to run the risk of failure. They know that sooner or later they will reach their goals if they keep trying.

BE A GOAL SETTER – Successful people plan for the future. They use goals as a personal road map to guide them where they want to go. By setting goals, people are able to realize their dreams.

ALWAYS BE POSITIVE – Be aware of a negative attitude in yourself and others. You should avoid those with a negative attitude.

REMEMBER – When you blame somebody else for your troubles, you have automatically given him or her power.

The longer I live, the more I realize the impact of attitude on life. Attitude to me is more important than facts, more important than the past, than education, than money, than circumstances, than failures, than success, than whatever people think, say, or do. It is more important than appearance, talent, or skill. It will make or break a company or a home. The remarkable thing is that we have a choice every day regarding the attitude we will embrace for that day. We cannot change the inevitable. The only thing we can do is play on the one string we have, and that is our attitude. I am convinced that life is 10% what happens to me and 90% how I react to it. And so it is with you. We are in charge of our lives.

—Charles Swindol

Pencils

A PENCIL MAKER TOLD THE PENCIL 5 IMPORTANT LESSONS JUST BEFORE PUTTING IT IN THE BOX:

1.) EVERYTHING YOU DO WILL ALWAYS LEAVE A MARK

2.) YOU CAN ALWAYS CORRECT THE MISTAKES YOU MAKE

3.) WHAT IS IMPORTANT IS WHAT IS INSIDE OF YOU

4.) IN LIFE, YOU WILL UNDERGO PAINFUL SHARPENINGS, WHICH WILL ONLY MAKE YOU BETTER

5.) TO BE THE BEST PENCIL, YOU MUST ALLOW YOURSELF TO BE HELD AND GUIDED BY THE HAND THAT HOLDS YOU.

"We all need to be constantly sharpened. This parable may encourage you to know that you are a special person, with unique God-given talents and abilities. Only you can fulfill the purpose which you were born to accomplish. Never allow yourself to get discouraged and think that your life is insignificant and cannot be changed and, like the pencil, always remember that the most important part of who you are is what's inside you.

Maybe they aren't pencils, after all …"

—Anonymous

The Pencil was patented in 1858

"Continuous effort, not strength or intelligence is the key to unlocking our potential."

—Winston Churchill.

Chapter 6

Goal Setting and Affirmations

Goals

A GOAL is the ongoing pursuit of a worthy objective until Accomplished!

"ONGOING" means it is a process because GOALS take time.

"PURSUIT" indicates a chase may be involved. There will likely be some obstacles and hurdles to overcome.

"WORTHY" shows that the chase may be worthwhile, that there is a big enough reward at the end to endure the tough times.

"UNTIL ACCOMPLISHED" suggests you will do whatever it takes to get the job done.

<u>You Can Live Your Dreams</u>

Your present situation does not determine where you can go,

It merely determines where you are starting from.

The purpose of a GOAL is to focus your attention on your future.

Real magic begins when you set one.

Your power to accomplish anything

Becomes a reality when you have a GOAL.

Your mind will stretch toward achievement when it has a clear objective.

—Anonymous and revised

> It has been said, "If you can imagine it, you can achieve
> it! If you can dream it, you can become it."

You Are So Blessed

(Something to Think About)

If you woke up this morning with more health than illness, you are more blessed than the million people who won't survive the week.

If you have never experienced the danger of battle, the loneliness of imprisonment, the agony of torture, or the pangs of starvation, you are ahead of 20 million people around the world.

If you attend a church meeting without fear of harassment, arrest, torture, or death, you are more blessed than almost 3 billion people in the world.

If you have food in your refrigerator, clothes on your back, a roof over your head, and a place to sleep, You are richer than 75 percent of this world!

If you have money in the bank and in your wallet, and spare change in a dish someplace, you are among the top 8 percent of the world's wealthy.

If your parents are still married and alive, you are very rare, especially in the United States.

If you can hold your head with a smile on your face and are truly thankful, you are blessed because the majority can, but most do not.

If you can hold someone's hand, hug them or even touch them on the shoulder, you are blessed because you can offer God's healing touch.

If you can read this message, you are more blessed than over 2 billion people in the world who cannot read anything at all.

YOU ARE SO BLESSED IN WAYS YOU MAY NEVER KNOW!

—Anonymous

Famous People with Learning Disorders and Other Disabilities

Celebrity	Disability	Celebrity	Disability
Jim Abbott	missing forearm and hand	Greg Louganis	LD
Hans Christian Anderson	LD	Steven McQueen	*
Beethoven	deaf	Mozart	*
Harry Belafonte	*	Patricia Neal	aphasic
Julius Caesar	epilepsy, seizure disorder	Louis Pastuer	*
Ray Charles	blind	Gen. George Patton	LD
Cher	LD, dyslexic	Ronald Reagan	hard of hearing
Winston Churchill	LD	Richard the Third	scoliosis
Norm Crosby	hearing and speech disability	Eddie Rickenbacker	*
Tom Cruise	LD, dyslexic	Nelson Rockefeller	LD
Leonardo Da Vinci	*	Franklin D. Roosevelt	polio (paraplegic)
Tom Demsey	missing toes	Theodore Roosevelt	visually impaired
Walt Disney	LD	Charles Schwab	*
Patty Duke	manic depressive	George C. Scott	*
Thomas Edison	deaf	George Bernard Shaw	*
Albert Einstein	LD	Tom Smothers	*
Dwight D. Eisenhower	*	Suzanne Somers	dyslexic
Henry Ford	*	Sylvester Stallone	*
F. Scott Fitzgerald	*	Mel Tillis	dysfluent
Galileo	*	Jules Verne	*
Danny Glover	epilepsy	Werner Von Braun	LD
Whoopi Goldberg	LD	Lindsay Wagner	*
Alexander Graham Bell	LD	Bree Walker	ectrodactylism
Bruce Jenner	LD	Gen. Westmoreland	*
Magic Johnson	HIV positive	Robin Williams	ADHD
Helen Keller	blind and deaf	Henry Winkler	*
John F. Kennedy	back brace	Woodrow Wilson	LD, dyslexic
Robert Kennedy	*	Wright Brothers	*
John Lennon	*	Wrigley	*
Carl Lewis	*		

*Indicates ADHD, LD, or ADD

Self-Esteem

Appreciating my own

worth and importance and

having the character to be

accountable for

myself and to act

responsible for others!

Going through challenges with a positive attitude enhances self-esteem!

Five Steps to Build Self-Esteem

The following steps will help you build your self-esteem:

1. Be yourself. Be real. Be honest.

2. Accept and love yourself.

3. Believe in yourself—believe you can do it.

4. Take responsibility for yourself. The choices you make will determine the course of your life.

5. Take action. Life is not what happens to you, it is what you make happen.

A person with high self-esteem feels capable and competent; takes responsibility for self; responds warmly to others; likes self and others; compliments others; takes risks, initiative, and action; gives honest description of own strengths; and accepts constructive criticism.

Also, use affirmations daily. Affirmations are positive statements about yourself and what you want. They start with "I am or "I will" or "I have." Say what you are, what you want, and where you want to be as if it already is!

> It has been said, "The greatest discovery of any generation is that human beings can alter their lives by altering their attitudes."

—William James

Affirmations

Affirmations start with "I am …"

Affirmations are positive.

Affirmations are short, specific, and about yourself

Affirmations need words that end in "ing." For example, "I am *living* in a big beautiful house *overlooking* the water."

Say what you are, what you want, and where you want to be as if it already is!

"Call those things that are not as though they already are" (Romans 4:17).

Repeat your affirmations daily.

Affirmations are now, like faith is now!

"Faith is the substance of things hoped for and the evidence of things not seen" (Hebrews 11:1).

In order to be successful, you need to do the following:

- forget your past
- replace negative talk with positive talk
- take charge of your thoughts
- say "I can" instead of "I can't" (words are power)
- know your personal strengths (if someone hurts you, be quick to forgive)
- stop complaining and blaming others
- do what you say you are going to do (be accountable)
- be willing to change / broaden your horizons
- use good judgment
- stay in school
- plan your future / decide what you want
- stay focused

"You create your own destiny as you go along."

—Winston Churchill

Goals

A goal needs to be attainable and measurable, as well as

- something you really want,
- something you can see yourself doing,
- specific (saying how much and by when),
- something you believe you can obtain,
- something that will not hurt anyone else,
- something you are willing to pay the price for (in time and effort), and
- identified as a short-term or long-term goal (e.g., I will own a new white Lexus by June 2022).

Move out of your comfort zone. If you do what you have always done, you will get what you have always gotten. (Many have made that statement.)

People who don't have goals end up being used by people who do!

"To have eyes and no vision is worse than being blind."

—Helen Keller

Action

If you want to do something, do it now!

Ask

If you want something, ask. Stay persistent! If you have nothing to lose but being embarrassed, ask!

If fear keeps you from asking, just admit you are afraid. Remind yourself of all the other scary events you have lived through in your life.

If you are afraid of doing something, just do it afraid.

It has been said, "FEAR is False Evidence Appearing Real."

We should not let our fears hold us back from pursuing our hope. (John F. Kennedy)

Don't be afraid. Just trust me. (Mark 5:36)

Risk

Risks must be taken if you desire to succeed. The person who risks nothing has nothing. Sometimes we have to step out to find out!

Time Management

Everyone has twenty-four hours in a day. How you spend your time is up to you. In order to have good time-management skills, you must learn to set priorities. Go to bed later or get up earlier. Do your chores and responsibilities and then go have fun. Everyone has priorities. People always say, "I am too busy" or " I did not have time."

"Excuses are all reasons stuffed in a lie."

—Joyce Meyer

Attitude

Life is 10% of what happens to you and 90% of how you react to it.

Every day is a brand-new day. We can wake up and choose to be in a good mood or in a bad mood. We all look in the mirror every day, so start talking to the mirror! Say positive confessions and attributes about yourself every day. You know yourself better than anyone else. It takes twenty-one to thirty-one days to make or break a habit. The more you say what you are, the more you will believe it and become it. For example, I am confident, kind, dependable, a team player, enthusiastic, organized, a leader, creative, fast learner, responsible, always take initiative, and have great management skills.

Persevere: Never Give Up!

Everyone has problems at some time in his or her life. The only ones who don't are in the cemetery or in heaven. Try to look at your problems as an opportunity to work out for your good.

No matter how hard it is and how long it takes, be persistent!

Benjamin Franklin, Businessman, Inventor, and Diplomat

Benjamin Franklin said about misspelled words, "A person who only knows how to spell a word one way is very uncreative."

Obstacles and/or mistakes he overcame were

- he had less than two years of formal schooling,
- he ran away from home as a teenager, and
- he started his apprentice printing career penniless and unknown.

What he achieved through perseverance was

- he became a master printer and owner of his own newspaper,
- he proved that lightning is a form of electricity, and
- he taught that a poor man can achieve success through hard work, thrift, and honesty.

He also once said, "If you do for a man what he can and should do for himself, you are doing him a disservice."

Walt Disney, Entrepreneur and "Imagineer"

Obstacles and/or mistakes he overcame were

- he was rejected as a cartoonist because he wasn't good enough, and
- he went bankrupt five times.

What he achieved through perseverance was

- he developed the Mickey Mouse cartoon character,
- conceived the idea of the Disneyland theme parks and built them in spite of skeptics,
- developed the ideas for Disney World Florida and the international versions, and
- brought happiness to millions of people around the world.

Jackie Robinson, Baseball Star

Obstacles and/or mistakes he overcame were

- his father left the family when Jackie was six months old,
- Jackie joined a gang as a teenager, and
- he received hate mail and death threats as a black baseball player.

What he achieved through perseverance was

- he was the first black player in professional baseball,
- his success in baseball opened up all professional sports to other black athletes, and
- he is remembered for saying, "A life is not important except in the impact it has on other lives."

Former Presidents

If at first you don't succeed, you're in good company.

Abraham Lincoln (1861–1865)

Abraham Lincoln's first business, a dry goods store, was a flop. He was later appointed postmaster in his township and had the worst efficiency record in the county.

Franklin D. Roosevelt (1933–1945)

Franklin D. Roosevelt began his career in public service after flunking out of Columbia Law School. He then decided to run for governor of New York.

Dwight D. Eisenhower (1953–1961)

Dwight D. Eisenhower was rejected three times for command positions before being appointed supreme allied commander in 1942.

Harry Truman (1945–1953)

Harry Truman opened a hat and shirt shop at age thirty-five that went bankrupt after just two years. Truman worked fifteen years to pay off the debt.

Our greatest glory consists not in never falling, but rising every time we fall.

The Farmer and His Donkey

One day a farmer's donkey fell into a well. The animal cried piteously for hours as the farmer tried to figure out what to do. Finally, he decided the animal was old and the well needed to be covered up anyway. It just wasn't worth it to retrieve the donkey.

So he invited all his neighbors to come over and help him. They all grabbed a shovel and began to shovel dirt into the well. At first, the donkey realized what was happening and cried horribly. (Sound like anyone you know? "I just feel like everything is coming in on top of me, shovels of dirt and junk."

After awhile, to everyone's amazement the donkey quieted down. A few shovel loads later, the farmer looked down and was astonished at what he saw. With each shovel of dirt that had hit his back, the donkey was doing something amazing: he shook it off and stepped on top of it.

As the farmer continued to shovel dirt on top of the donkey, the donkey shook it off and stepped on top of it.

Pretty soon, everyone was amazed when the donkey stepped up over the edge of the well and trotted off!

When you have a trial and get upset, you can't hear from God! You have to hold onto your peace and be calm inside.

Life is going to shovel dirt on you, all kinds of dirt. The trick to getting out of the well is to shake it off and take a step up. Each of our troubles is a stepping-stone. We can get out of the deepest well just by not stopping, never giving up! So shake it off and take a step up.

Positive Affirmations

Zip up your negative thoughts and only confess the positive!

Following are some positive thoughts you might try and say out loud:

- I am in control of my life and am here for a purpose.
- I choose to be successful.
- I am a great person and have great potential.
- I can have whatever I say and believe.
- I will complete every task I start.
- I have rock-solid confidence in my abilities.
- I have friends who genuinely care about me.
- Everything I do will prosper, and I have the power to get wealth.
- I reject blame and negativity.
- I have the capacity to _____.
- I will be a _____ by 2022 or _____.
- I am productive, organized, focused, and have great time-management skills.
- I love myself.
- I will earn an honest living.
- I choose to take responsibility for my life.
- I have a great future.
- I am full of supernatural energy.
- I am an excellent listener and have great communication skills.
- I will be early and on time, everywhere I go.
- I have wisdom and choose friends who are wise.
- I honor my word and keep my promises.
- I have a good sense of humor and keep things in perspective.
- I am getting better and better every day in every way.
- I can follow as well as lead—I am a good team member.
- I am persistent, generous, loving, kind, and unique.
- I feel good about myself, and my self-esteem is growing.
- I am intelligent, creative, and have common sense.
- I look good, I feel good, and I weigh _____ pounds.
- I have developed a personal mission statement for my life.
- I have earned the respect of others, and they consider my word my bond.
- I forgive freely rather than hold grudges.
- I refuse to judge other people and their values.
- I exercise good moral and ethical influence on others.

- My business standards are no different from my personal standards.
- I have the courage to meet any challenge life may present.
- I am selective with the thoughts that fill my mind.
- I only eat healthy snacks, such as fruit, between meals.
- I go to my doctor, dentist, and eye doctor at least once a year.
- I have power, love, and a sound mind.
- I drink at least six to eight glasses of water a day.
- I keep commitments to myself and others.
- I am special and feel good about myself.
- I was created to be prosperous, successful, and wealthy.
- I am selective on whom I date and will marry.
- I will not doubt or fear what I can achieve.
- I believe in me and can do what I set my mind to.
- My life is characterized by joy and satisfaction.
- I am blessed and highly favored.
- Today is my set time for favor.
- I am coming out of this valley.
- The healing power of Jesus is working in me right now.
- A shift is coming in my life.
- What God has in my future will supersede what is in my past.
- My best days are in front of me.
- My future will be brighter and better.
- This is my set time for freedom and healing.
- I have the authority by the grace of God to be healed.
- I have all the resources for my success.
- I am out of poverty and living my dreams.
- Money is looking for me.
- I am whole and sound in every area of my life.
- I am destined for the good life.
- God is on the throne and fighting my battles.
- I have increased favor and divine connections.
- I walk, talk, and live in faith every day.
- God wants me to prosper in every way.
- I am blessed going in and blessed going out.
- God has made me a blessing so I can be a blessing.
- I am acting, speaking, and believing "as if."
- I believe I receive the good life now.
- Faith is my response to what God has already provided.
- The Universe is conspiring good to me every day.
- This is my receiving day.
- Every day is my receiving day.

Select some you like or choose your own and say a few each and every day. Watch your life transform. I say some of these each morning in the shower and use some biblical scriptures too. It takes twenty-one to thirty days to form a habit. Making positive confessions daily can manifest powerful outcomes. Here are my favorites:

"I can do all things through Christ who strengthens me" (Philippians 4:13).

"Faith is the substance of things hoped for and the evidence of things yet not seen" (Hebrews 11:1).

(Romans 4:17) "Says to call those things that be not as though they are".

"The joy of the Lord is your strength" (Nehemiah 8:10).

If you are not saying anything, you may not be creating anything.

"You must learn a new way to think before you can master a new a way to be."

— Marianne Williamson

Some Keys to Success

Acknowledge Your Positive Past

Appreciate the things about you that make you the person you are. That includes your successes, your family background, and the struggles you have survived. Acknowledge the skills and strengths you have developed to apply to your job. If you have had a bad experience at a former job, look at what you learned from that experience. The past is to learn from, not to live in.

Positive Self-Talk

Make sure that your self-talk is positive. We are like computers—the things we say over and over again to ourselves are the things we believe and will act upon. If you keep saying, "I can't work because …," you are giving additional power to obstacles and keeping yourself trapped in a system that enables you to be dependent. Eliminate words like *can't*, *try*, *I have to*, and *they made me*. These take away your power. Instead, use phrases like "I can," "I will," and "I choose."

Acknowledge Your Strengths

Many people do not acknowledge their strengths because they have been taught that it is conceited to do so. However, being able to acknowledge your strengths is what will help you do well in any scary situation, such as a job interview. If you get along well with people, use that strength to face the situation. It also helps to know your strengths when an employer asks, "Tell me about yourself." If you respond with modesty, you don't give the employer a reason to hire you. You need to be confident.

Clarify Your Vision and Value

In order to *get* what you want, you first have to *know* what you want. Daydream about what it is you would like to do. Daydream as if you had no limitations. Close your eyes and see yourself working. Be specific. What kind of work are you doing? Are you working inside or outside? Are you working with people or alone? Dreams and visions can become very powerful!

Plan Your Future

Once you have a dream about what it is you want to do, make a plan as to how you are going to get it. Take baby steps. Develop a written action plan. Your goals must be something you can see yourself doing. They must be specific. Say how much and by when. Here are some examples: (1) I will have a full-time clerical position with the county by April 1, 2020; and (2) I will save $10.00 a week for the next year ($520.00!).

Visualize and Affirm Your Success

In order to achieve your goals, you must be able to see yourself as having already accomplished them. This is a proven technique that successful athletes have used. They don't see themselves running the race; they see themselves running through the finish line tape. See yourself happily working in the type of job you want. Use positive affirmations, such as, "I am proudly working as a medical assistant" or whatever it might be. (Watch *The Secret* or read the book.)

Act to Create It

If you want something, do whatever it takes to get it. Be willing to pay the price with action and determination. If you need more education to get a job promotion, take one class a quarter at night school or online until you are eligible for the promotion. If you need to lose weight, start by cutting out the junk! Then take baby steps toward your weight-loss goal.

Respond to Feedback

Listen and act upon feedback you get from other people. If you keep applying for jobs without getting hired, and people tell you that you need to wear a tie to get the job, don't argue how you don't need to wear a tie to fix a computer. Start wearing a tie!

Persevere

You have to "keep on keeping on" no matter how tough it gets. People who find jobs are the ones who do not give up. The successful job hunter is the one who treats the job search as a full-time job. It may take several no's before you get the yes you want. However, if you give up, you'll miss out on it altogether.

Reap the Rewards

Reward yourself when you have achieved your goal. Take yourself shopping, on a vacation, or whatever makes you feel good!

We are what we repeatedly do. Excellence, then, is not an art but a habit. (Aristotle)

Important Goals by Category

(Write your responses)

My #1 personal goal is

My #1 business goal is

My #1 self-development goal is

My #1 financial goal is

My #1 family goal is

My #1 mental goal is

My #1 social goal is

My #1 spiritual goal is

My #1 physical goal is

"All dreams can come true if we have the courage to pursue them."

—Walt Disney

Vision Board or Book

Put a picture board together or a notebook. (Need vision plus action.)

Look at your visions and goals often. Some of the following are outlined in *The Secret*:

- Hold it in your hands and really internalize the future.

- Read your affirmations and inspirational words out loud.

- See yourself living in that manner.

- Feel yourself in the future you have designed.

- Believe it is already yours.

- Be grateful for the good that is already present in your life.

- Acknowledge any goals you have already achieved.

- Acknowledge the changes you have seen and felt.

- Acknowledge the presence of God in your life.

- Acknowledge the law of attraction at work in your life.

- Look at it just before going to bed and first thing upon rising.

See it, feel it, believe it!

Speak it, visualize it, and view it! Set your intention on attaining it!

"If you can mold it in your thoughts, you will eventually hold it in your hands."

—Jerry Savelle

Bill Bartmann's Nine Steps to Achieve Any Goal

Bill Bartmann left home at age fourteen, lived under a bridge, ate out of Dumpsters, joined a street gang, became an alcoholic at age seventeen, and was close to suicide. He spent five years in high school and did not graduate. Even the US Marines did not want him. Now he is a successful speaker and millionaire and a testimony to others. Following are the steps he created to achieve any goal:

1. Make sure it is your own goal.

2. What do you think about when you think about goals? Change to "promise."

3. Identify your promise.

4. Identify your personal motivation.

5. Create a promise plan.

6. Review your plan regularly.

7. Tell yourself you are going to achieve this.

8. Tell others.

9. Envision, project the result, and see yourself there. Take your dreams to bed.

Be sure to review this process twenty minutes daily, stay focused, and make a list of your notable accomplishments.

Guiding Questions in Assisting Someone to Pursue Their Dreams

by

Denise Bissonnette, author, job developer, poet, and curriculum developer.

Printed with permission.

1. Why do you want this? What do you imagine will be different in your life as a result of following through on this dream?

2. What factors need to be considered in pursuit of this dream? Such as, timing, money, information, planning, support, etc.

3. What strength / skills / resources do you need to pursue the dream?

4. What are the possible obstacles you may face in pursuit of this dream? What small steps could you take to remove those obstacles?

5. Are you committed to this dream? If not, what would have to happen in order for you to commit to following through on it.

6. What would be the cost to you of not pursuing through on it?

7. What are 5–10 small steps you could take in the next week that could bring you closer to bringing this dream into fruition / reality?

8. Which of those 5–10 small steps are you willing to be accountable for in the next week?

* Think about some of your childhood dreams and consider the piece of truth each held regardless of whether or not it came true.

* "Vision isn't enough unless combined with venture. It's not enough to stare up the steps unless we also step up the stairs." (Vance Havner)

What Is Success?

To laugh often and much,

To win the respect of intelligent people and the affection of children,

To earn the appreciation of honest critics and endure the betrayal of false friends,

To appreciate beauty;

To find the best in others,

To leave the world a bit better, whether by a healthy child, a garden patch or a redeemed social condition;

To know even one life has breathed easier because you have lived;

"This is to have succeeded."

—Ralph Waldo Emerson

Three Ways to Change Your Life

It has been said that there are three easy ways to change your life. They are:

1. Keep doing what works,

2. Stop doing what doesn't,

3. Start doing what will!

And if you change the way you look at things, you will change the way you see things.

Chapter 7

Employment and Educational Resources

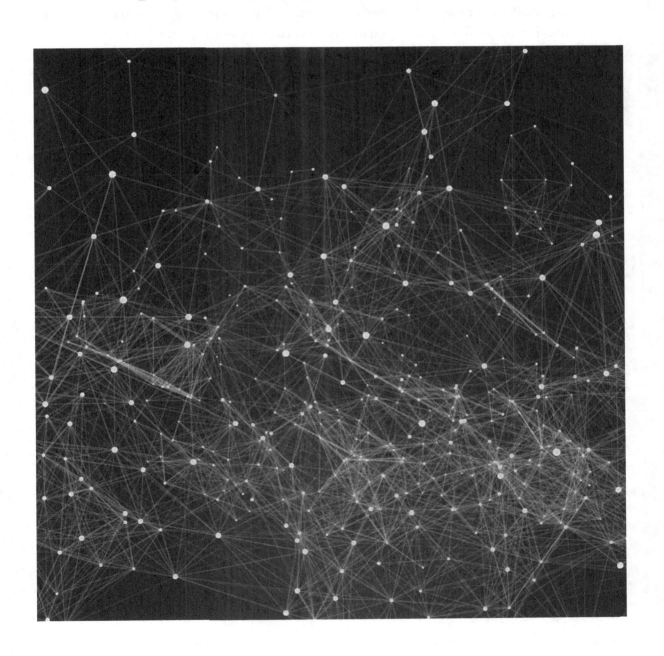

Tips for Participating in Job Fairs

You do not have a second chance to make a good first impression! Do the following to ensure that you do so:

1. Dress professionally. Wear a suit if possible. Handle this as you would a regular interview. Always dress to impress!

2. Wear comfortable shoes. Lines are frequently long and you should expect to wait, especially for some of the popular companies. Bring a sample application with you that is already filled out so you can just transfer the information.

3. Résumés. Bring a supply to hand out to the companies.

4. Take a portfolio, briefcase, or file folder to hold résumés and corporate literature.

5. Prepare a "one-minute commercial." Think about your strong points and goals, the company, and where you want to go within the company.

6. Be prepared to discuss where you want to work geographically, what you like doing and are looking for in a job, and your most relevant skills.

7. Arrive early. Plan on extra time for checking in. Leave kids at home!

8. Network. While you are waiting in line, talk to others. You may hear about opportunities you were not aware of.

9. Be assertive and show initiative. Shake hands and introduce yourself to the employers and recruiters when you reach the table.

10. Be enthusiastic. Employer surveys identify that the single most important personal attribute applicants can bring to a position is enthusiasm. So smile and project interest in the company.

11. There will be many applicants approaching employers at the same time you are. Don't be overwhelmed by the experience. Keep a positive attitude, and concentrate on the benefits of the experience.

12. Explore options. A wide variety of companies will normally participate. This is an excellent opportunity to browse and indulge your curiosity. You can walk around first and see who you want to approach.

13. Make sure to write down the companies you applied with and whom you spoke to. Then later you can make your follow-up calls. Get business cards if available.

Apprenticeship Information

STATE OF CALIFORNIA

DEPARTMENT OF INDUSTRIAL RELATIONS

DEPARTMENT OF APPRENTICESHIP STANDARDS

28 Civic Center Plaza, Room 525

Santa Ana, CA 92701

(213) 576-7750

IT PAYS TO BE AN

APPRENTICE

If you have a high school diploma, you can go on to career training while you earn a living by getting into a California apprenticeship program.

The apprenticeship system (practical on-the-job training combined with related classroom instruction) differs from other kinds of training by it being firmly based on an employee-employer relationship, in which the apprentice receives. Apprenticeship programs vary in length from one to five years with most running an average of two to four years.

An apprentice is a full-time paid employee who learns an occupation at the worksite as well as in the classroom. The apprentice works for a salary that increases as each higher skill level is successfully completed. At the end of an apprenticeship the State of California awards a Certificate of Completion, signifying that the individual has completed training which meets the industry standards for the particular occupation. This certificate is recognized throughout the industry as a valid indicator of high-quality training.

Apprenticeship Standards cover the terms and conditions for the apprentice's employment and training. The apprentice signs an agreement with either the employer or an administrative committee that he or she will attend school on their own time. In exchange the employer will provide them on-the-job training in the trade. In addition the employer signs an agreement with the State that they will train that individual in the selected work process of the trade. And upon satisfactory completion of each level will provide regular graduated pay increases as the apprentice becomes more proficient. This agreement is then filed with the Division of Apprenticeship Standards.

STATE OF CALIFORNIA

DEPARTMENT OF INDUSTRIAL RELATIONS

DEPARTMENT OF APPRENTICESHIP STANDARDS

28 Civic Center Plaza, Room 525

Santa Ana, CA 92701

(213) 576-7750

<u>Apprenticeship</u>

ANSWERING YOUR QUESTIONS ABOUT IT

APPREINTICESHIP: In the simplest terms, is training in occupations that require a wide and diverse range of skills and knowledge, as well a maturity and independent judgment. It involves planned day-by-day training, on-the-job experience under proper supervision, combined with related instruction.

THE APPRENTICE: Is usually a high school graduate of legal working age, with a manual dexterity and other characteristics directly related to the apprentice occupation to be learned.

LENGTH OF TRAINING: Varies depending on the occupation and is determined by standards adopted by the industry. The minimum terms for an apprenticeship is about one year.

APPRENTICEABLE OCCUPATIONS: Can be found in such industries as electronics, construction, service, metal working and medical and health care. There are many occupations that are recognized by the Division of Apprenticeship Standards.

RELATED INSTRUCTION: Covers such subjects as mathematics, blueprint reading, applied English and other technical courses needed for the specific occupation, and is customarily taken outside working hours.

ON-THE-JOB TRAINING: Is the learning of each process by caring it out step by step under the close supervision of a skilled craft worker (journeyman).

WAGES: Paid to the apprentice begin at approximately half those of the fully trained journey level craft worker and usually advance at 6 to 12 month intervals until the apprentice completes the training. Then the apprentice will advance to the full journey level wage.

APPRENTICESHIP PROGRAMS: May be sponsored by an employer, a group of employers, or a union. (Often employers and unions form a committee which determines industry needs, the kind of training required, and set the standards required acceptance into the program).

Hospital-Based Health Care Careers to Consider

1. **Admitting Clerk**:

   In-Patient, Out-Patient, and Emergency Department. High school education with office skills to include typing, filing, etc.

   Medical terminology beneficial.

   PBX Operator:

   Telephone skills required with office skills preferred.

   High school education.

2. **Dietary**:

   Kitchen, cafeteria, food lines, dishwashing. High school education preferred.

   Certification classes.

   Registered Dietician: Emphasis on patient education skills related to special diets, for example with diabetic and cardiac patients.

   College degree in nutrition.

3. **Housekeeping/Environmental Services**:

   Responsible for all aspects of hospital cleaning, linen services, trash disposal. High school education preferred.

4. **Data Processing**:

    Responsible for computer programming and use, assisting staff with computer usage. Some college required; varies with position.

5. **Accounting:**

    Patient billing services, general accounting. High school education.

    College education preferred; varies with position.

6. **Engineering/Maintenance**:

    Responsible for service, repair, and maintenance of hospital equipment and facility. High school education; experience preferred.

7. **Medical Records**:

    Responsible for patient record keeping including medical

    Transcriptions, filing, microfiche. High school education with office skills including typing and filing. Knowledge of medical terminology preferred.

8. **Human Resources/Personnel Services:**

    High school education with office skills including filing and record keeping.

9. **Purchasing:**

    Responsible for maintenance of hospital supplies.

    High school education preferred.

    Laboratory Technician:

    Responsible for laboratory testing. College degree plus internship.

10. **Phlebotomist:**

    Responsible for blood drawing for lab tests. High school education, training programs available at community colleges or technical school level.

11. **Radiology Technician:**

    Responsible for x-ray diagnostics. College degree plus internship.

12. **Respiratory Therapist:**

    Responsible for therapy related to respiratory management.

    Community college or four-year college degree.

    EKG Technician:

    Community college certification.

13. **Physical Therapist:**

    Responsible for therapy related to physical activity levels including ambulating and exercise. College degree.

14. **Pharmacist:**

Responsible for provision of prescribed drugs and solutions. College degree plus pharmaceutical certification.

Pharmacy Technician:

Provision of supportive service to pharmacist. High school education.

15. **Social Worker:**

Provide counseling and referral to patients related to social needs.

College degree.

16. **Medical Staff Office:**

Responsible for record keeping and program provision for physician staff. High school education with office skills including shorthand, typing, and filing.

17. **Administrative Secretarial Position:**

High school education with office skills.

18. **Nursing:**

Registered Nurses (2-6 years college), Licensed Vocation Nurses (12-18 months college), Certified Nurses Aide (community college or technical school certification or experience), runner, ward clerk (high school education with clerical skills).

Areas for Nursing: Medical/Surgical, Obstetrics, Intensive Care, Mental Health, Oncology, Operating and Recovery Room, Emergency, Pediatrics, IV Therapy, Resource Management, Administration, and Education.

Related ROP courses are as follows:

Medical Assistant–Front Office; Prerequisite: Medical Terminology
Medical Assistant—Back Office; Prerequisite: Medical Terminology
Medical Assistant Review; Prerequisite: Medical Assistant Front and Back
Medical: EKG Monitor Technician; Prerequisite: Medical Terminology
Medical: Health Care Occupations
Medical Insurance Billing; Prerequisite: Medical Terminology
Medical: Introduction to Health Care Careers and Medical Terminology
Medical Phlebotomy Technician; Prerequisite: high school diploma or GED
Physical Therapy Aide
Medical Terminology
Emergency Medical Technician
Introduction to Vocational Nursing
Nurse Assistant / Home Health Aide (CNA)
Pharmacy Technician

Menu of Jobs Available in the Restaurant Industry

There are several opportunities for employment in the restaurant industry. They are as follows:

1. Banquet manager. Plans and oversees parties, banquets, conventions, and other special events hosted or catered by the restaurant.
2. Bartender. Responsible for the setup, maintenance, and operation of the bar.
3. Broiler cook. Responsible for all grilled, broiled, or roasted items prepared in the kitchen of a foodservice establishment.
4. Bus staff. Serves water, bread, and butter to guests and refills water glasses as needed; removes dirty dishes between courses; clears, cleans, and resets tables after customers leave.
5. Dining room manager. Directs dining room and coordinates foodservice activities. Also maintains payroll, bookkeeping, and food and beverage records.
6. Executive chef. This department head is responsible for any and all kitchens in a food-service establishment.
7. Expediter. Functions as the communications link among the various food-production areas in the kitchen.
8. Fry or sauté cook. Responsible for all fried or sautéed items prepared in the kitchen of a foodservice establishment.
9. General manager or unit manager. Maintains overall management responsibilities for the foodservice establishment.
10. Human resource manager. Recruits and hires qualified employees, creates in-house job-training programs, and assists employees with their career needs.
11. Kitchen manager. Supervises and coordinates activities concerning all back-of the-house operations and personnel operations and personnel, including food preparation and kitchen and storeroom areas.
12. Maitre d'hôtel. Manages the dining room, schedules and supervises the waitstaff, hosts, and bus staff.
13. Pantry cook. Responsible for all cold food items prepared in the kitchen of a foodservice establishment.
14. Pastry chef. Responsible for the pastry shop in a foodservice establishment.
15. President or CEO. Manages the entire restaurant operation. Responsible for running a profitable and successful business.
16. Public relations manager. Helps the restaurant create and maintain a positive image; publicizes fundraisers, parties, special discounts, and other newsworthy events.
17. Server. Describes menu and daily specials, takes orders, serves food, and makes sure that customers have everything they need to enjoy their meal.

18. Soup and sauce cook. Responsible for all soup and sauces prepared in the kitchen of a foodservice establishment.
19. Sous chef. The sous chef acts as second in command in the kitchen, directing and managing cooks and other kitchen workers; takes over when the executive chef is absent.
20. Wine steward. Selects and orders the wine for the restaurant; teaches staff how to describe, recommend, and serve wine to customers.

Farmers Insurance

Information provided by an Insurance agent.

It has been said, "The insurance industry makes up 80 percent of the wealth in the United States."

FARMERS OPPORTUNITY:

- Residual Income—one of the greatest inventions in the world
- The ability to control your own destiny—be your own boss
- Unlimited Income Potential—Top Agents earn $1 million + a year
- Build equity in your business—Contract Value
- Family Rights Provision—pass your business on to your family
- Job security (own your own agency without fear of corporate lay-offs)
- Recession Proof
- Unlimited pool of prospects

ABOUT THE POSITION:

Farmers Insurance is a dynamic and widely respected group of insurance companies. Agent stated that they are one of the largest Property and Casualty insurance companies in America. Their product line is unmatched in the industry. They are also a leading force in the commercial insurance market and provide invaluable Life Insurance and Financial Services to millions of Americans.

This is not employment, but rather an opportunity to build your own business without all of the large start up costs. This is like a franchise without the franchise fee. They are looking for qualified people that have the vision of starting a career versus looking for another job. The support and the comprehensive training program they offer are second to none.

SKILLS / REQUIREMENTS:

When selecting agent candidates, they look for those individuals who are:

- Motivated with an entrepreneurial spirit
- Have a Strong Work Ethic and are self-motivated
- Good Credit History
- No Bankruptcies in the last 3 years
- No criminal convictions or felonies
- Responsible driving record
- Bilingual a plus, but not required

If you want an opportunity to own a business and be your own boss, create job security, and live life on your own terms, being a Farmers insurance agent is that opportunity.

For more information, contact your local District Manager at any Insurance Office.

Guard Cards

The steps to acquire a guard card are as follows:

1. Must be eighteen years old and pass a criminal background check.
2. Complete eight hours of the forty hours CA guard card course.
3. Prices range from $60–$75. Guard card training locations can be found on the guard card website.
4. Take and pass the "Power To Arrest" Course—must pass with 100%. (Open-book test!!)
5. Complete guard card application and send to CA Bureau of Security Investigative Services.
6. Visit "Live Scan" for fingerprinting. They will submit to California Department of Justice (DOJ).
7. Wait to receive card in the mail. Takes seven to ten days.

Online guard card: www.onlinesecurityschool.com

Security certification: Schools.com/Security

Security guard training: Campuscorner.com/Security

Securitas: www.securitasjobs.com – They hire often!

* Must make an appointment! There are two classes and two sets of prints required, one for the FBI, the other for the DOJ.

Total for classes, fingerprinting, live scan, and guard card is usually $225. (Check in your area.)

The ETPL has a list of guard card training programs at http://etpl.edd.ca.gov/wiaetplprog.asp

QUESTIONS AND ANSWERS ABOUT ROP

HISTORY

The San Bernardino County Superintendent of Schools Regional Occupational Program was organized in 1973 by the County Superintendent's Office and a group of ten participating school districts. The SBCSS ROP is accredited by the Western Association of Schools and Colleges (WASC).

WHAT IS THE PURPOSE OF THE REGIONAL OCCUPATIONAL PROGRAM?

The ROP provides open entry, open exit career technical education and support services that augment and expand the capabilities of our school districts. Our courses provide instruction for entry-level employment, advanced training, and upgrading skills. ROP courses are limited to occupational areas where there is reasonable expectation of employment or postsecondary articulation, and where there is sufficient student interest.

HOW MANY DISTRICTS ARE SERVED BY THE SBCSS ROP?

There are currently sixteen secondary districts:

Apple Valley • Baker Valley • Barstow • Bear Valley Fontana • Hesperia • Lucerne Valley • Morongo Needles • Rialto • Rim of the World • San Bernardino City Silver Valley • Snowline • Trona • Victor Valley

Two other ROPs serve the following county school districts:
Colton, Redlands, Yucaipa - CRYROP (909) 793-3115
www.cryrop.k12.ca.us
Chaffey, Chino Valley, Claremont, Upland -
Baldy View ROP (909) 624-0063 www.baldyviewrop.com

HOW IS THE ROP ADMINISTERED?

The San Bernardino County Superintendent of Schools employs a director and staff to oversee the budget, develop instructional programs and to provide support services within ROP operational guidelines. The San Bernardino County Superintendent of Schools ROP is organized on a decentralized basis contracting with districts to run individual programs that meet local student and employer needs. Each district manages the day-to-day operation of the courses they offer. Our governance structure consists of a Board of Directors made up of the County Superintendent of Schools and the superintendents of the sixteen member districts and Coordinating Council, an advisory body composed of district representatives.

HOW IS THE ROP FUNDED?

The ROP has an average enrollment of 14,000 with a base Average Daily Attendance (ADA) of 2,238. Apportionment funds (ADA) are received from the state to finance its operations. Each program is designed to be self-supporting based on funding received from student hourly attendance. Lottery dollars are also allocated based on ADA and used to purchase new equipment and materials. No federal funds are included in the ROP operational revenues.

This ROP does not charge tuition; however, students may be required to purchase certain materials and books which they can keep. Unless specifically noted otherwise, students will be responsible for providing their own transportation to class locations including community classroom sites.

WHO ATTENDS ROP CLASSES?

Depending on the policies of the member district, any high school student over 16 or adult may attend an ROP class offered in any district served by our ROP. **To maintain the original concept of ROP, high school students receive priority in enrolling in any class; however, adults are welcome on a space-available basis.** Travel distance is the only limitation on inter-district attendance.

WHO ARE THE ROP INSTRUCTORS?

ROP instructors are specialists from business and industry chosen for their expertise and experience in their particular subject field. Each instructor is credentialed by the California Teaching Commission and is required to complete designated teaching methodology classes.

WHERE ARE THE ROP CLASSES OFFERED?

ROP classes are offered either on local campuses and/or in local businesses where potential employment actually exists. Community facilities and equipment are utilized under formal agreements signed by the business representative and the County Superintendent of Schools to provide a combination of school site and work site learning.

WHEN ARE ROP CLASSES OFFERED?

Most ROP classes are offered during the day to meet the needs of high school students, adults and our participating businesses. Some classes are offered in the evening to accommodate working adults.

CAN SCHOOL CREDIT BE EARNED FOR TAKING ROP CLASSES?

High school students who satisfactorily complete the course requirements can be granted credit according to local district policies. ROP students completing a course receive a Certificate of Competency, which is signed by the instructor. In addition, many classes are articulated with local community colleges.

WHAT IS MEANT BY ARTICULATED CLASSES?

Articulation is an agreement between the ROP and community colleges or four-year colleges which allows a student to receive some type of credit towards a college course for competencies learned in the ROP courses.

DOES THE ROP OFFER GUIDANCE AND COUNSELING SERVICES?

The San Bernardino County Superintendent of Schools ROP offers a variety of services to potential and enrolled ROP students. These support services include career and educational counseling, career assessment, career planning assistance, educational and occupational information and job search placement assistance.

ARE EMPLOYERS INVOLVED WITH THE ROP?

Employers support the ROP in a variety of ways. Through their participation on advisory committees, business leaders assist in verifying local labor market demand, determining curriculum content, providing expert consultants and recommending qualified instructors. In addition, employers provide facilities, equipment, and promote student job placement.

California Picture ID Cards

When you do not have a driver's license, you need to get an official ID card to prove who you are. It is best to start this process before leaving high school because your high school ID will expire. You must have an ID for employment. Anyone of any age may apply for an ID card: children, seniors, and non-drivers. A regular ID card is good for six years. To acquire an ID, take the following steps:

Step 1. Visit or make an appointment at your local DMV office. Online services are not available for this process. You will need an original DL44 form. You can have this sent to you before your appointment or fill it out at the DMV.

Step 2. When you arrive at the DMV on your appointment day, be prepared to fill out the application form DL44. You will have your picture taken and your thumbprint. You will need to provide your social security number and proof of birth date and legal presence. Then pay your fee.

Step 3. Before you leave the DMV, make sure they have your correct current mailing address. Your ID will be mailed to you within sixty days and as fast as two weeks. If you have not received your ID after sixty days, call your local DMV office at 1-800-777-0133. Hearing Impaired: TTY (800-368-4327). For website information: WWW.DMV.CA.GOV

The fee for an original ID card, a renewal ID, or a replacement, name-change, or emancipated minor ID is $28.00. A reduced-fee ID card is $9.00. You will need form DL937. You can obtain that from your public assistance program or provider. (Fees are subject to change.)

Items needed before applying for an ID are

- driver license or identification card application form DL44. The DL44 is not available online because original signatures are required and each form contains a unique barcode that must be scanned by DMV employees.

- an acceptable birth-date or legal-presence document. State law requires every applicant to show verification of birth date and proof of legal presence within the United States. If your current name no longer matches the name on your birth-date or legal-presence document, see "True Full Name" and "How to Change Your Name" for more information. Only the original or a certified copy of some of the following documents is acceptable (see website for other documents):

US birth certificate
US Certificate of Report of Birth Abroad
birth certificate or passport issued from a US territory
US passport
US military identification card
Certificate of Naturalization or Citizenship
INS US citizen ID card
permanent resident card
temporary resident ID card

- your social security number. Proof of your social security number is not required. Your number will be verified with the SSA while you wait.

- your true full name. Your true full name appears on your birth-date or legal-presence document. If you change your name, you must provide a name-change document to verify your name change, such as adoption documents that contain the legal name as a result of the adoption; any name-change document that contains the legal name both before and after the name change; marriage certificate; dissolution of marriage or partnership document that contains the legal name as a result of the court action; or a certificate, declaration, or registration document verifying the formation of a domestic partnership.

CAL Grants: Money for College

Cal Grants Awards guaranteed for students who qualify.

College is now more affordable than ever for students with good grades and financial need. The best part is that Cal Grant cost nothing to apply for and does not have to be repaid!

Students who meet the following criteria are guaranteed grants:

Cal Grant A Entitlement Awards

- Requirements include financial and basic eligibility (see box lower right), and a minimum 3.0 grade point average (GPA). Students must apply by March 2nd either the year they graduate from high school or the following year. This entitlement Award provides for fees at the California State University and the University of California, as well as tuition support at private California colleges and universities.*

Cal Grant B Entitlement Awards

- Requirements include financial and basic eligibility and a minimum 2.0 GPA. Students must apply by March 2nd either the year they graduate from high school or the following year. This Entitlement Award provides up to $1,551 for books and living expenses for students in their first year of college.

For the second and subsequent years, the award also helps pay for tuition and fees at the California State University and the University of California, as well as tuition support at private California colleges and Universities.*

California Community College Transfer Entitlement Awards

Students who meet financial and basic eligibility requirements, have a minimum 2.4 GPA from a California Community College, were California Community College, were California residents when they graduated from high school, and graduate from high school July 1, 2000, or later are eligible for this award when transferring from a community college to a four-year institution.

This Entitlement Award is offered to California Community College students who were not awarded a Cal Grant within a year of graduating from high school, but meet certain eligibility requirements at the time of transfer from a California Community College to most four-year colleges or universities in California.

Basic Cal Grant eligibility requirements

All Cal Grant applicants must:
- Basic Cal Grant eligibility requirements
- All Cal Grant applicants must:
- Be California residents
- Be U.S. citizens or eligible non-citizens
- Meet U.S. Selective Service Requirements
- Attend a qualifying California postsecondary institution
- Be enrolled at least half-time
- Maintain satisfactory academic progress as defined at the school of attendance
- Have family income and assets below the established ceilings
- Not be in default on any student loan
- Not owe any federal or state grant refund

Everyone should apply

All students are encouraged to apply for financial aid, even if their family income and assets are above the ceilings.

Many things can happen, between the time the FAFSA is submitted and the start of school that can dramatically change a family's situation, including illness or layoff.

Other Cal Grant Programs

Cal Grant A and B Competitive Awards

Students who are not eligible for a Cal Grant A or B Competitive Award.

These awards are similar to the Cal Grant A and B Entitlement Awards, except that they are not guaranteed. Each year, 22,500 awards are available. Of these, 11,250 awards are available to students to students who do not qualify for an Entitlement Award, but who file by the March 2 deadline and meet Competitive eligibility criteria. These criteria are geared toward nontraditional students and take into consideration family income, parent's educational level, GPA, time out of high school, high school performance standards and other factors, such as whether the student comes from a single-parent household or is a former foster youth.

California Community College students can compete for the remaining 11,250 awards during September 2nd application deadline period.

Cal Grant C Awards

Cal grant C Awards are available to assists students with tuition, fees and training costs for occupational or vocational programs. The $576 Cal Grant C Award provides for books, tools, and equipment.

Students planning to attend a school other than a California Community College may also receive up to $2,592 is assistance.

To qualify for Cal Grant C Awards, students must meet basic eligibility requirements and be enrolled in a vocational program that is at least four months in length.

For more information on Cal Grants

Visit the California Student Aid Commission Web sites at: www.csac.ca.gov or www.calgrants.org Call the Commission's Student Support Service staff at: 888-224-7268 (that's 888-CA-GRANT) Write us at: California Student Aid Commission P.O. Box 419027 Rancho Cordova, CA 95741-9027 Email us at: studentsupport@csac.ca.gov For a list of Cal Grant eligible schools: Log on to the Commission's Web site and click on: Search for a Cal Grant Eligible School To find income and asset ceilings: On the Commission's Web site, click on income and Asset Ceilings

How to apply for a Cal Grant!

To apply for a Cal Grant, students must do two things: Submit a Free Application for Federal Student Aid (FAFSA) **and** File a Grade Point Average (GPA) Verification Form, or make sure their high school or college has filed the GPA on their behalf. When to apply – Each January 1st starts the application period when students can file their FAFSA online at www.fafsa.ed.gov or file a paper FAFSA. Students may obtain a paper FAFSA from their high school counselor or college financial aid office or download it from either of the Commission's two Web sites, at left.

Deadlines-Both the FAFSA and GPA Verification form must be submitted, or post-marked, no later than March 2nd. California Community College students have a second chance to apply by the September 2nd deadline.

Get a FAFSA PIN now: To file as FAFSA online, each student needs a personal identification number, or pin, and the parent of a dependent student needs a PIN, too.

Students and parents may log onto the internet, go to www. fafsa.ed.gov, then, click on Getting Started and follow the prompts. It's fast and easy.

Employment City

Following are some occupations to ponder. Where there is a need, there is a job!

accountants / bookkeepers, tax services, banking

actors, artists, authors, music careers

appliance, furniture, and moving companies

assembly-line jobs

automotive: truck drivers, insurance companies

aviation: planes, flight attendants, airport jobs

cabinetmakers, cable installers

chiropractic, massage

construction: carpentry, homes, painting, etc.

cosmetology: hair, nails, beauty supplies

day care centers, nannies

delivery services drivers

dental, eye care

electricians, welders, plumbers, bridge builders, tile setters

engineering, drafting, mining

firefighters

fish and game, water-sport jobs

floral, funeral parlors, makeup artists

gyms: exercise and dance instructors

heating and air-conditioning

hospitals: nursing, doctors, pharmacy techs

hotel industry: housekeeping, human resources

landscaping, forestry jobs

law: attorneys

machine operators

motorcycle repair techs, bike repair

newspapers, publishers

office jobs

police, security guards, prison jobs

pools and spas

postal jobs, government jobs

real estate agents, loan officers, property management

repair places

restaurants, foodservice industry

retail: clothing, food, shoes, jewelry, merchandise

road workers

schools: teachers, bus drivers, therapists, counselors

ski areas

sports, lifeguards

TV or radio, camera operators, marketing, sales

technology, IT tech support, phones, computers

tour guides, photographers

trains, cruise lines, shipyards, boat docks

vets, animal care, groomers

warehouse, distribution

Web designers, architects

… and the list goes on …

Employment Websites

Local and Inland Area and More

Please research the following website for even more employment opportunities.

www.indeed.com/jobs

www.co.san-bernardino.ca.us/

www.caljobs.ca.gov/

www.dvmc.com/dvmc/group/employment/index.asp

www.mthigh.com/employment/index.html

www.snagajob.com/

www.highdesertjobs.com/monster/

www.constructionjobs.com/index_eng.cfm

www.workcircle.us/jobs

www.edjoin.org

www.themallofvictorvalley.comjobs.asp

www.realcaliforniajobs.com/index.aspx

www.allretailjobs.com/

www.monster.com

www.jobonline.com

www.careerbuilder.com

www.job-hunt.org

www.simplyhired.com

www.JobsRadar.com

www.Job.com

www.flipdog.com

www.jobcentral.com

www.learn4good.com/jobs

www.rileyguide.com

www.worktree.com

www.nationjob.com

www.kaiserpermanentejobs.org

www.thejobspider.com

www.christianjobs.com

www.online.onetcenter.org

www.usajobssite.com

www.jobweb.org

www.employment911.com/asp/JobSeekersEnter.asp

www.thingamajob.com

www.yourjobstop.com

www.k12jobs.com

www.seniorjobbank.com

www.alljobsearch.com

www.PerfectLocalJobs.com

www.theonlinebeat.com/employment

www.jobsearchsite.com

www.postjobs.net

www.sbcounty.gov

www.GoCoastGuard.Com

www.ntc-iapws.com (IAP—World Services)

https://chart.donhr.navy.mil

www.rayjobs.com (defense and government)

www.ga-asi.com (General Atomics)

www.LASD.ORG (LAPD)

www.mojavewater.org

www.usa.jobs.gov

www.timewarner.com/corp/careers

www.Ralphs.com

www.sbcss.k12.ca.us

www.AirJobsDaily.com

www.AirJobsDigest.com

www.Jet-Jobs.com

www.careers.bestbuy.com

www.cityofhesperia.us

www.dot.ca.gov (Cal Trans)

www.fedex.com/us/careers

www.betterhighdesertjobs.com

www.jobdirect.com

www.lowes.com/careers

www.basicedservices.com (tutoring K–12)

www.SCE.com

www.target.com/careers

www.jobsinlogistics.com

www.verizon.com/careers

www.ruscareers.com

www.upsjobs.com

www.tsa.dot.gov

www.overseasjobs.com

www.softwarejobs.com

www.continental.com

www.wellsfargo.com

www.boeing.com

www.disney.com

www.internships.com

www.kellyservices.com

www.cbs.com

www.showbizjobs.com

www.paramount.com

www.co.la.ca.us (County of LA)

www.usajobs.opm.gov (federal jobs)

www.healthcaresource.com

www.ritzcarlton.com

www.careerjet.com

www.coachhelp.com (football coach)

www.computerwork.com

www.connectme.com

www.starchefs.com (culinary jobs)

www.electricalengineer.com

www.ejobs.org (environmental jobs)

www.espn.com

www.layover.com (truck-driver jobs)

www.vjf.ocm (virtual job fair) or www.virtual-job-fair.com

www.worldjobmat.com

www.careers.citifinancial.com

www.lowes.com/careers

www.CDCR.ca.gov

www.mthigh.com

www.mining-technology.com/jobs/career/job-ladder.html

www.dot.ca.gov (Caltrans)

www.fs.fed.us/fsjobs/index.shtml (US Forest Service jobs)

www.edisonjobs.com

www.collegehlepers.com

www.nettemps.com

www.Samplinginstore.com

www.acinet.org (state and local labor market data)

www.servicelocator.org (Connects to local offices that provide training.)

www.workforcetools.org (Helps gain knowledge and skills to excel at jobs.)

www.online.onetcenter.org (detailed descriptions of occupations)

www.jobshadow.org

Able Forces	http://ableforces.org/employment.opportunities/
Account Temps	www.accountemps.com
Adelanto School District	www.adelanto.k12.ca.us/
Aerospace Network	www.aerospace.net
AFG	www.afg.com
AMC Theaters	www.amctheatres.com
Apex Bulk Commodities, Inc.	www.apexbulk.com
Apple Valley Science Tech Center	www.avstc.org
Apple Valley Unified School Dist.	www.avusd.org/
Apple Valley, Town of	www.applevalley.org/
Aviation/Aerospace	www.nationjob.com/aviation
Barstow Community College	www.barstow.cc.ca.us
Barstow Unified School Dist.	www.barstow.k12.ca.us

Barstow Community Hospital   www.barstowhospital.com

Bear Valley U. School Dist.   www.bigbear.k12.ca.us

Best Buy   www.bestbuy.com

Boeing Home Page   www.boeing.com

Border Patrol   http://www.honorfirst.com/

Burlington Northern Santa Fe   www.bnsf.com/

California Conservation Corps   www.ccc.ca.gov

CA City Guide 2000   http://www.cacities.org/

CA State Dept. Corrections

CA State Personnel Board   http://jobs.spb.ca.gov/

CA Dept. of Personnel Admin.   http://www.dpa.ca.gov/

Cal Jobs (can access @EDD)   www.caljobs.ca.gov

CA Labor Market Info   http://www.calmis.cahwnet.gov/

Cal State San Bernardino   www.csub.edu/

CA State Assoc. of Counties   http://csac.counties.org/

Cal Trans   www.dot.ca.gov or http://jobs.ca.gov

Census Bureau 2000   http://www.census.gov

Central Intelligence Agency   http://www.cia.gov

Charter Communications   www.charter.com

Certified Registered Nurses   www.crnaemployment.com

Chino Unified School Dist.   www.chino.k12.ca.us/

Cinemark Theaters   www.cinemark.com

City of Adelanto	www.adelanto.com
City of Barstow	www.barstow.ca.com or http://www.barstowca.org
City of Claremont	www.ci.claremont.ca.us
City of Chino	www.ci.chino.ca.us
City of Colton	www.ci.colton.ca.us
City of Fontana	www.fontana.org
City of Hesperia	www.ci.hesperia.ca.us
City of Loma Linda	www.ci.lomalinda.ca.us
City of Montclair	www.ci.montclair.ca.us
City of Ontario	www.ci.ontario.ca.us
City of Redlands	www.ci.redlands.ca.us
City of Rialto	www.ci.rialto.ca.us
City of Riverside	www.ci.riverside.ca.us
City of San Bernardino	www.ci.san-bernardino.ca.us
City of Upland	www.ci.upland.ca.us
City of Victorville	www.ci.victorville.ca.us
Computerwork.com	www.computerwork.com
Coca Cola	www.enjoycareers.com
Costco / Price Club	www.pricecostco.com
Daily Press	www.highdesert.com
Desert Valley Medical	www.primecare.net
Desert Valley Hospital	www.dvmc.com

DICE—Technology	www.dice.com
Disneyland	www.disney.com
DOJ attorney job listing	http://www.usdoj.gov/gopherdata/oapm/index.html
Drug Enforcement Admin.	http://www.usdoj.gov/dea/job/ads.htm
EDD	http://www.edd.ca.gov/
Engineering employment	www.interec.net/
Enterprise Rent-A-Car	www.goenterprise.com
FBI	http://www.fbi.gov/employment/employ.htm
FCC jobs	http://www.fcc.gov/jobs/
Fed Jobs Central	http://www.fedjobs.com/
Federal Jobs Digest	http://jobsfed.com/
Federal Government Jobs	http://federaljobs.net/
Government Jobs	http://www.governmentjobs.com
Pro Gov Jobs	http://www.govjobs.com/index.htm
Gov Central	http://www.govcentral.monster.com
United States Secret Service	http://www.treas.gov/usss/index.htm?opportunities.htm&1
USA Jobs	http://www.usajobs.opm.gov/
Fontana U. School Dist.	www.fusd.net/employment/index.stm
Heilig Meyers Corp	www.heligmeyers.com
HireAbility.com	www.hireability.com
Home Base	www.homebase.com
Pharmajobs (international)	www.pharmajobs.com/

IT job openings	www.dice.com/register
Job Source Inc.	www.Job-Source.com/
Kaiser Hospital	www.medimatch.com/
Kelly Temp Services	www.kellyservices.com
Kmart	www.kmart.com
Labor Ready	www.laborreready.com/
Lockheed Martin	www.lmco.com
Loma Linda University MC	www.llu.edu/
Los Angeles Times	www.latimes.com
Los Angeles County	http://www.co.la.ca.us/
Lucerne Valley U. School Dist.	www.lvsd.k12.ca.us
Manpower Staffing Services	www.manpower.com/
Med America Billing Services, Inc.	www.medamericabilling.cm
Northrup Grumman Corporation	www.northgrum.com
Ontario airport	www.csz.com/ont.html
Ontario-Montclair School Dist.	www.omsd.k12.ca.us/
Orange County Register	www.ocregister.com
PepsiCo	www.pepsico.com/
Pluess Staufer, Inc	www.omya.com
Ralphs Markets	www.ralphs.com
Redlands Comm. Hospital	www.redlandshospital.com/
Redlands U. School Dist.	www.redlands.k12.ca.us/

Redlands University	www.uor.edu/
Riverside County	www.rc-hr.com or http://www.co.riverside.ca.us/
Riverside County of Education	www.rcoe.k12.ca.us/
Riverside U. School Dist.	www.rusd.k12.ca.us/
Riverside, University of CA	www.ucr.edu/
Riverside Press Enterprise	www.pe.com
Roadway Express	www.roadway.com
San Antonio Comm. Hospital	www.sah.org/
San Joaquin Valley College	www.sjvc.edu
SB Comm. College Dist.	www.sbccd.cc.ca.us/
SB County	www.co.san-bernardino.ca.us/ or www.sbcounty.gov
SB Supt. Of Schools	www.edjoin.org
SBU School Dist.	www.sbcusd.k12.ca.us/
San Bernardino Sun	www.sbcsun.com/
Select Personnel	www.selectpersonnel.com/
Silver Valley U. School Dist.	www.silvervalley.k12.ca.us
Snowline J. U. School Dist.	www.snowline.k12.ca.us
Southern CA Gas Corp	www.socalgas.com
State of CA homepage	http://www.ca.gov/
St. Mary Hospital	www.StMaryapplevalley.com
Target	www.target.com/
TechJobBank	www.techjobbank.com/

The Mall of Victor Valley	www.themallofvictorvalley.com
Thomas Staffing	www.thomas-staffing.com/
TV jobs	www.tvjobsusa.com
UPS	www.ups.com
United Security Services	www.unitedweguard.com
Victor Valley Comm. College	www.vvc.edu or www.vvcforme.com
Victor Valley Global Medical Center www.vvgmc.com	
Victor Valley School Dist.	www.vvuhsd.k12.ca.us/
Victor Valley Transit Authority	www.vvta.org
Vons Markets	www.vons.com
Wackenhut Corrections	www.wackenhut.com
Walmart	www.wal-mart.com
White House internships	http://whitehouse.gov/internship/
Yellow Freight Systems, Inc.	www.yellowfreight.com

* If a website is not listed next to the name, just type the name of the company in the search box.

Job Fairs

Jobs America Expo dates and locations

http://www.jobsamerica.com/jalocations2001.html or just www.jobsamerica.com

Type "job fairs" in the search box and click "LA Job Fairs/Employment Guide." You will see jobs from LA to across the country.

Los Angeles Times Job Fair

http://www.latimes.com/class/employ/fair/

Orange County Register's Career Fairs. Click "Jobs."

http://www.ocregister.com/employment/smartcareerfair.shtml

http://www.edd.ca.gov/Jobs_and_Training/Job_Fairs_and_Events.htm

California Jobs, Websites, and Resources

Following is a listing of employers that hire often and are in high demand:

- DirecTV and other cable companies (always need tech support people)
- airports
- police departments: LAPD. JOINLAPD.COM or call (866) 444-LAPD. For seminars and tests call (661) 949-6543 or 800-A Deputy. www.LASD.ORG also for security.

Explorer Program: Ages 14–21 S.B. (909) 387-0641

Or http://www.co.san-bernardino.ca.us/sheriff/volunteer/volunteer.asp

Citizens Patrol: (909) 387-0641 or www.cosan-bernardion.ca.us/sheriff

- Securitas Security: www.securitasjob.com
- security officer: www.LASD.ORG
- correctional officer: https://www.usajobs.gov/
- schools
- fire departments: www.sbcfire.org
- SB County Fires Department Explorer Program: (909) 829-4441
- hospitals
- restaurants
- real estate agents
- military (US Army accepts ages 17–42.)
- Avon and other cosmetic companies (Be your own boss.)
- apprenticeships: (213) 576-7750 or (213) 576-7750
- dir.ca.gov/databases/das/aigstart.asp
- apprenticeship electrician: (909) 890-1703
- power lineman: (951) 685-8658
- Associated Builders Contractors (ABC): (714) 779-3199
- The Laborers School: (626) 610-1700 or (877) 445-2094
- Schwan Food: www.theschwanfoodcompany.com
- skilled utility workers, warehouse, distribution, rail, trucking, transportation, and logistics
- chauffeurs (age twenty-five or older with clean DMV; need to know freeways and directions)
- truck drivers
- Ashley Furniture truck drivers: www.ashleyfurniture.com or (800) 837-2241
- tutoring K–12 all over: www.basicedservices.com
- alarm companies (always looking for sales people)

- Federal Bureau of Prisons: www.bop.gov/jobs/
- General Atomics: http://www.ga-asi.com
- Caltrans highway maintenance: www.spb.ca.gov
- BNSF Railway: www.bnsf.com
- insurance companies (become an agent)
- Utiliquest (They locate underground utilities and cover a wide demographic area including Arizona.) (951) 682-0777. Must be eighteen with a good driving record.
- United States Postal Jobs: www.usps.com
- United Health Group:
- https://careers.unitedhealthgroup.com/getting-hiredtransitioning-military
- UPS (shortage of drivers): (888) 967-5877 or UPSJOBS.COM
- Tanger Outlet Mall in Lennwood / Barstow (always hiring): http://www.tangeroutlet.com/barstow/careers
- San Bernardino County (always looking for qualified candidates): http://www.co.sanbernardino.ca.us/main/working.asp or http://www.sbcounty.gov/hr
- Riverside County (always looking for candidates): http://agency.governmentjobs.com/riverside/default.cfm
- warehouse opportunities: http://www.warehousejobs.com/

Seasonal Hires

The following jobs usually start in September but sometimes in the spring:

Halloween stores

pumpkin patches

Christmas tree lots

ski resorts and marinas

H&R Block

UPS

fairgrounds

Santa Claus and Easter Bunny (check your malls)

Youth Employment

The following jobs are great for high school and college students:

sign holders

pizza delivery drivers

volunteering

fast food restaurants

retail and grocery stores

child care, golf caddies, and movie theaters

vacation and tourism spots

parks and recreations / youth programs / lifeguards

campgrounds

museums

zoos

moving companies

pool cleaners

construction Jobs / helpers

check out job fairs

check with school career centers

start your own business

car washing, lawn and yard care

events planner

errand service for the elderly

personal shoppers

garage sale organizers

home/closet organizers

recruiting travel agents for medical jobs, etc.

pet and house-sitters

technology services

tutoring

street curb addressing

auto services (including bikes and skateboards)

Christmas tree lighters in your neighborhood

use hobbies as a job, make flyers

Following are some jobs that may pay you to see the world:

1.   Roadie. Musicians are always looking for people who have strong backs who can set up equipment and take care of lighting and sound check. Visit EntertainmentCareers.net.
2.   Diplomat/foreign service officer with the US State Department. Need to be age twenty and pass the Foreign Service exam. The government pays the officers to learn a new language and take culture classes.
3.   Cruise ship crewmember. Luxury cruise lines always looking to fill all sorts of jobs.
4.   Rail worker
5.   Amtrak riders. You could get paid to write your novel while living on a train.
6.   National park workers
7.   Tour bus drivers
8.   Flight attendants
9.   Traveling nurses
10. Truckers
11. Recruiters (various types)
12. Nannies
13. Fitness instructors

Following are websites for jobs for teens:

Summerjobs.com

CoolWorks.com

Campjobs.com

Teens4Hire.org

Myfirstpaycheck.org

GroovJob.com (Taco Bell)

SimplyHired.com (This also helps with child care jobs.)

SnagAjob (Enter your zip code.)

InternJobs.com

Internships.com

Monster, Career Builder, and Indeed

Social networks: LinkedIn, Twitter, and Facebook. Employers also look for you. Be careful what is on your profile! You may have to clean it up under Privacy settings. You want to make sure to use a professional photo and have an elevator pitch about yourself.

Here are some schools and training programs to help prepare you for your career:

- Fashion Institute of Design and Merchandising (FIDM)
  Location: Los Angeles: (213) 624-1201 or (800) 711-7175
  Orange County: (714) 565-2800
  San Diego: (619) 235-2049
  San Francisco: (415) 675-5200
- School of California Arts/Pasadena: (866) 227-0881 or www.csca.edu (closing)
- The Art Institute of California SB: Artinsitutes.edu or (800) 870-2073
- Mackay School of Earth Sciences and Engineering: www.unr.edu/mackay/studentservices
- ROP (check with local high schools)
- Diplomas: Pennfosterhighschool.com
- Life After High School
- SJVC private junior college: consumerinfo.sjvc.edu

- Westech College: www.westech.edu
- California Conservation Corps: Ages 18–25, (800) 952-JOBS or WWW.CCC. CA.GOV
- Job Corps: ages 16–24, (800) 733-JOBS or http://recruiting.jobcorps.gov
- US Truck Driving School: (800) 519-7364
- A+ certifications. Study and take test: ExamCollection.com
- Online GED preparation course: http://MAXEDUCATION.ORG
- Health care documentation program specialists and vocational online course for billing, coding, transcription, and report editing: www.at-homeprofessions.edu or call (877) 515-5110
- Health Coaches are now in huge demand!
- Health Coach Institute / San Francisco: (877) 914-2242

Other areas of employment to consider are

- Schneider National Logistics, transloading and distribution. www.Schneider.com
- retail opportunities. http://www.allretailjobs.com/
- Home Depot, Inc. https://careers.homedepot.com
- Penske driving and warehousing. www.PenskeLogistics.com
- Petsmart. http://careers.petsmart.com
- Best Buy. www.Best Buy.com/careers
- Big5 Sporting Goods. Big5sportinggoods.com/careers
- Walmart Distribution Center. www.walmartstores.com
- Goodwill Southern California. www.goodwillcocal.org
- Mars Company. http://www.mars.com/global/careers/job-search.aspx
- National Park Service. http://www.nps.gov/personnel/main_trade.htm
- Dr. Pepper / Snapple. www.dpsg.com/careers or www.drpeppersnapplegroup.com
- Red Cross. www.americanredcross.apply2jobs.com
- Edison. www.sce.com/CTAC or http://www.edison.com/home/careers.htm
- Southwest Gas. https://careers-swgas.icims.com/jobs/intro
- Geo Group, local and global jobs. http://thegeogroupinc.com/carees.asp
- cities and counties
- TJX Companies Inc. Employment references guide for TJ Maxx, Marshalls, Home Goods, and Sierra Trading Post locations: http://www.tjx.com/contact_locator. asp#8panel1-1
- NAF and civil service jobs. www.cpol.army.mil
- OmniTrans. http://www.omnitrans.org/about/jobs.asp
- Staffing agencies in your area. Staffmaker in SB, Fontana, and Riverside (951) 351-4192 or www.staffmark.com
- Labor Ready temporary labor. Work today and get paid today. Offices in all states over 800 locations: (800) 245-2267 or www.LaborReady.com
- ICR. www.ICRJob.com or (888) 244-5802

- tutoring. Xamaze Tutoring: One-on-one tutoring service working with students K–12.
- Apply at http://xamaze.com/become-a-tutor or call (800) 581-8045.
- tutoring. Nonprofit education organization since 1972, serving students throughout California. Apply at TUTORS@ASAPCAL.COM
- tutoring. www.ElevateLearningUSA.Com/Tutor. Pays $16–$20 per hour.

Following are websites for other information regarding employment:

- worker rights: www.dir.ca.gov or www.workitout.ca.gov
- http://www.keepyourhomecalifornia.com/
- EDD unemployment: www.labormarketinfo.ca.gov
- tax credit forms for employers / WOTC: www.edd.ca.gov/worcind.htm
- Phone: (866) 593-0173 or http://www.irs.gov/pub/irs-pdf/i8850.pdf
- California New Start Program / Prerelease Program: http://www.edd.ca.gov/Jobsandtraining/pubs/osfile.pdf
- food handler cards: http://www.sbcounty.gov/dehs
- social security: (800) 772-1213
- DMV: (800) 777-0133 or WWW.DMV.CA.GOV
- student aid: www.fafsa.gov
- Job Search Assistant Worksmart: www.worksmart.ca.gov
- America's Job Center: http://jobcenter.usa.gov/
- Springboard counseling: www.credit.org
- Department of Rehabilitation: http://www.dor.ca.gov/
- orientation for the blind: ocbinfo@dor.ca.gov or www.dds.ca.gov
- Inland Regional Center: (909) 890-3273 or (909) 890-3000
- Limited Examination and Appointment Program (LEAP) is designed to help facilitate the recruitment and hiring of people with disabilities. https://jobs.ca.gov/Job/Leap
- Rolling Start, CA, independent living centers. Assist people with disabilities
- San Bernardino, CA: (909) 890-9516; Hesperia, CA: (760) 949-7626
- http://www.rehab.cahwnet.gov/ils/ILC-List.html
- online resources for serving special populations students: www.jspac.org
- RetirementJobs.com
- Seniors4hire
- tools for career exploration: www.labormarketinfo.edd.ca.gov
- occupational outlook book. Find job and career information online
- www.bls.gov/oco/home.htm
- The Career Zone (assess yourself): www.cacareezone.org
- Who Do U Want 2B?: whodouwant2b.com/
- When You Turn 18: A Survival Guide for Teens: www.calbar.ca.gov/public/pamphlets/

- www.stopbullying.gov
- DREDF. Transition planning for students with disabilities and online resources on transition: info@dredf.org or www.dredf.org
- Glassdoor website has great employment tips: http://www.glassdoor.com
- suicide prevention. Hotline: (800) 273-8255. Or info@suicidology.org or www.suicidology.org

Following are links for study information for CAHSEE, GED, and SAT, as well as other educational links:

- SAT practice questions: www.testprepreview.com/gedlonks.htm
- Reviews algebra, sentence structure, writing, punctuation, measurement, essay writing, and more. Great to study for the CAHSEE or GED!
- CAHSEE practice test questions: www.cde.ca.gov/ta/tg/hs/resources.asp
- www.cde.ca.gov/ta/tg/hs/elaguide.asp
- www.cde.ca.gov/ta/tg/hs/documents/math06rtq.pdf
- GED information: www.ged123.org
- www.ede.ca.gov/ta/tg/gd/gedfaq.sp
- practice test for GED, SAT, and more: www.4tests.com
- online dictionary: www.dictionary.com
- Ask any question and receive a list of related links on the Internet that answer your questions: www.ask.com
- Online encyclopedia is updated daily with new information: www.wikipedia.org
- math homework: www.math.com
- www.algebrahelp.com
- algebra work: www.algebrahelp.com/calculators
- fractions help: www.helpwithfractions.com
- College Navigator: www.thecollegenavigator.com
- FAFSA. Free application for federal student aid: https://fafsa.ed.gov
- Princeton Review: www.princeton review. Test preparation and college admission services company that offers test preparation services, tutoring, and admissions resources.
- California trade schools: www.trade-schools.net

Here are some jobs in Fort Irwin, California:

- Northrop Grumman: www.norhtropgrumman.com or call (760) 380-2335
- AAFES: www.aafes.com or call (800) 508-8466
- IAP World Services
- Raytheon: www.raytheon.com/rcareeers
- Lockheed Martin global security: www.lockheedmartin.com/careers
- Westech International: www.westech-intl.com

- Serco. Provides contact employment in many locations of the world; connected with military locations: http://www.serco.com/
- Military Spouse Employment Partnership (MSEP): https://msepjobs.militaryonesource.mil/

Here are other websites to research for employment:

- Cal Jobs: www.caljobs.ca.gov or www.csb-wing.org or www.sbcounty.gov
- school education jobs: www.edjoin.org
- County of San Bernardino Workforce Development: https://www.csb-win.org/
- Cal Opps Public Employment Job Board: www.calopps.org
- ROP: WWW.ROP.CC (Check with your schools and area.)
- Career Builder.com (may be one of the best)
- HireMeNow.com
- Indeed
- JOBcentral
- Jobs.com
- Flipdog
- Monster.com
- SimplyHired
- SnagAJob
- USAJobs
- Zip Recruitor.com
- HighDesertJobs.com
- Soldiers4Hire (leaving the military): http://www.soldiers4hire.com/

The following government websites offer a wide variety of employment opportunities, with the last few specifically for veterans:

- www.federaljobsearch.com
- www.va.gov
- www.usajobs.com
- www.studentjobs.com
- www.caljobs.ca.gov
- https://jobs.ca.gov/
- www.va.gov/jobs
- www.vetjobs.com
- HireVetsFirst
- https://www.calvet.ca.gov/
- veteran website: https://www.vets.gov/veterans-employment-center/

And finally, please visit the following military websites, including the last three for ASVAB*:

- military transition: www.careeronestop.org/militarytransition. Links to key services for veterans and transitioning military personnel (CA and L).
- Military Spouse Employment Partnership (MSEP) (opportunities across the United States): https://msepjobs.militaryonesource.mil/
- www.asvab-practise-test.com
- www.military.com/ASVAB
- www.asvab.us/freeASVABtestonline.htm

*ASVAB (Armed Services Vocational Aptitude Battery)

Military and California Conservation Corps Information

Some graduating seniors have already passed the ASVAB test and are on their way into one of the military branches because they have planned for their future. That means they have an automatic job, paycheck, and place to live. There are a variety of jobs in the armed forces, and they provide many benefits, such as

- full pay and allowances during training,
- thirty days of paid vacation every year,
- advanced education at little or no cost,
- great retirement after twenty years of service,
- extra pay for certain types of duties and going overseas,
- free meals and housing or free dental and medical care,
- free or low-cost entertainment,
- regular promotions,
- savings when shopping at military stores,
- great opportunity to see the world and more, and
- jobs after service in the military.

The ASVAB is a timed multi-aptitude test developed and maintained by the Department of Defense. The ASVAB score varies with each military branch. You must meet the minimum score for each branch in order to be considered. The higher the scores, the more opportunities you will have.

Scores are in the areas of arithmetic reasoning, word knowledge, mathematics knowledge, mechanical comprehension, paragraph comprehension, English, and science. There are several books available to help you study for the ASVAB.

The California Conservation Corps (CCC)

The CCC is a paid training program for women and men ages 18–25. The CCC responds to emergencies, such as fires, floods, oil spills, hurricanes, earthquakes and other disasters.

Many high school students who do not go to college go into the CCC. Just as the military, it is an automatic job, pay, and place to live. The work is outdoors, and it is laborious. It does give individuals the opportunity to pursue other careers, such as working for Cal Trans and the fire department afterward. In other words, it opens other doors of opportunity. In addition, an individual can continue his or her education, earn scholarships for college, learn new skills, and travel. The pay may not be great but the experience is incredible.

Minimum qualifications are as follows:

- ages 18–25
- not on parole or probation
- no criminal convictions
- must be a CA resident
- pass fingerprint and background check
- willing to work outdoors
- willing to participate in emergency responses when required
- willing to participate in educational programs

Consider the difference you could be making while gaining valuable experience. They hire often! Contact the CCC at www.ccc.ca.gov or (800) 952-5627.

As you can see, there are no reasons to be unemployed if you can and want to work! But remember, some websites and numbers are subject to change, and the great thing about the Internet is that we can type in anything and it will usually come up.

It has been said, "Success isn't how far you got, but the distance you traveled from where you started".

There is no such thing
As Failure
If you Try

But what if I
Try & don't Succeed?
What do you call that?
LEARNING!

Anonymous

"Ninety-nine percent of all failures come from people who have a habit of making excuses."
George Washington Carver, chemist who discovered over 325 uses for the peanut.

Printed in the United States
By Bookmasters